The Pl

Issue

The Plays of Harold Pinter

Issues of Identity and Politics

Swarupananda Chatterjee

Prestige Books International
NEW DELHI

Published by
Prestige Books International
New Delhi 110 060
prestigebooks@gmail.com
Phone: 9818755529

Associate Office
London SW11 6HU

Associate Office
Sydney 2001

ISBN: 978-81-947512-3-6

Printed in India

Contents

Foreword

As we encounter the increasingly paradoxical nature of lived experience in the twenty-first century—what with the regimes of rightism ruling across the globe, the fraught politics of climate-change, a raging pandemic, the various precarities and migrations that unsettle the space of the subject—the plays of Harold Pinter acquire a relevance that cannot be overemphasized. It is almost as if his plays may be read as a symptom of the catastrophic, as a caveat to the impending apocalypse that categories of the human will face in a future world. Increasingly, one realizes how, the plays of Pinter anticipate a posthuman engagement with various forms of precarity—be it in *The Homecoming*, *The Birthday Party* or *The Room*. What were so aptly called 'comedies of menace' have acquired a newer relevance in an age and time qualified by techno-surveillance and the evolution of newer methodologies of control. The absurdity that lies at the heart of the Pinter play has more to do with the anxiety of the real than the etymological manifestations of the word 'absurd'. It is in the everyday that one encounters the menace, where the personal becomes the political and the lived moment is a dystopic implosion of the self. The very act of an encounter in the world of the Pinter plays is a moment of trauma laced with the uncertainty of any possibility of a normative faith in history, ethic or experience. Pinter addresses the crucial interface between the existential and the phenomenal where the self is defined in its terrible uncertainty facing a world that can never be recognized. The unknowability of the 'other' is severed from its Levinasian philosophical paradigm in Pinter's plays and is transformed into a political moment of unmitigated anxiety.

Swarupananda Chatterjee's book addresses this anxiety that vacillates between the uncertain interfaces of the existential and the phenomenal. In his analysis Chatterjee captures the spirit of some of Pinter's plays that define the modern condition in the susceptibility of the characters in the plays to a foundational anxiety of existence. The contingency that is at the heart of the modern condition is captured in Chatterjee's analysis when he locates identity within the ever-elusive web of the dynamic between the existential and the phenomenal. Through the paradigms of language and communication the author questions the fetish of meaning and locates this as a central problematic in his analysis of the Pinter plays. When language is reduced to a game, and identity to role-playing, the foundational notion of knowability is dismantled, and the social fabric that is predicated, ever so loosely, on the idea of relationships is unsettled. It is at this moment of confusion that Chatterjee brings in the question of power that operates through the ambivalent structures of certainty. Chatterjee deconstructs certainty through the lenses of identity and memory and discovers the impact of Pinter's plays in their analysis of the pervasive nature of power. The question of precarity is analyzed through the consuming act, in almost the entire oeuvre of Pinter's plays, of the unreliability that is at the heart of every human action. Action, the intrinsic part of a play, is held hostage at the inability or refusal of the characters to act. It is this horrifying self-reflexivity, the nature of which is a commentary on the narrative of the modern condition that Chatterjee sees as the crucial thrust in Pinter's technique. The centre cannot hold the spiraling explosion of meanings and the human subject is rendered helpless by the agency of non-human intervention. This is where Chatterjee anticipates the posthuman tilt in Pinter's work, and makes the reader rethink the possibilities that lurk behind conventional expectations of an absurdist play. The 'Who am I?' question is supplemented by the 'Where am I?' and the political force of the query becomes an important analytical tool of this book.

It is important to reiterate in this context that changes in literary trends have relegated absurdist plays, and therefore Pinter, to quiet corners of the academia. The revival of such voices is important in the context of the reiteration of the question of agency and how we choose to think about it in the context of the twenty-first century. It is imperative that we rethink questions of ontology, phenomenology and existentialism in the context of the techno-political nature of the world where we live today. The human question is still an important part of how we think about life on earth, and the failure of comprehension, that is the subject of most of Pinter's plays, is perhaps more relevant in the context of the present. The paratextual in Pinter breeds a menacing uncertainty, and this complex politico-ethical ploy undercuts what is 'present' in the play itself. This absent presence in the world of Pinter's plays is what helps us comprehend our world of pervasive absent presences—surveillance, climate change or cybernetics. A revisiting of Pinter's plays, a continuous reassessment, and possibly a re-fashioning in context is a necessary practice that needs to be sustained within literary studies. Chatterjee's intervention, therefore, is a relevant reminder to the student of literary studies of the continuing importance of close-reading Pinter in the classroom. There are, of course, many ways of reading Pinter, and Chatterjee's is only one of them. Also, I hope that the author takes up more plays for close-reading and analysis in the future, even if he is using the same tools and methodology for reading Harold Pinter's plays. A sustained engagement is crucial.

Sumit Chakrabarti
Professor, Department of English
Presidency University, Kolkata

Acknowledgements

Harold Pinter was one of the most renowned dramatists of the 20th century, esteemed for his originality and formal innovations. He is often bracketed with another Nobel Laureate Samuel Beckett, the great Irish dramatist. Both these writers dealt with the theme of existence and heralded a new movement, popularly known as the theatre of Absurd. Plays by these writers have been immensely popular in India and are widely prescribed in the syllabi of English literature curriculum. My reading some of Pinter's plays triggered my interest in the playwright. I was especially drawn be the issues of self, identity and the absurdity of modern man, a crucial concern for all of us.

The present book is based on my research project for M. Phil degree at Rabindrabharati University in 2013. Since the commencement of this work, I have been obliged to solicit the help and cooperation of numerous persons and institutions. It may not be possible to literally record my gratitude to all of them individually in a short space available here. But it remains treasured in the heart. I must, however, briefly acknowledge some of the scholars who constantly offered their guidance and support during the course of my research.

I express my deep sense of gratitude to Dr. Sumit Chakrabarti, Professor, Department of English, Presidency University whose painstaking supervision and valuable suggestions enabled me to prepare this project. Thank you, Sir, for all that concern and encouragement which helped me out whenever I got entangled in the labyrinth of critical plethora. Also, I am deeply obliged to all my revered teachers of the Department of English in Rabindrabharati University for their kind help and suggestions. My heartfelt gratitude to Dr. Bimlesh K. Singh, Head, Department of English, Mahatma Gandhi Central University, Motihari, who inspired me to get my research work published.

I owe a debt of gratitude to the staff of National Library, Calcutta and to that of the Central Library, Rabindrabharati University for their help in the collection of relevant research materials. Finally, a special thanks to Dr. Suman Bala and Dr. R.K. Dhawan of the University of Delhi for their editorial advice and to my publishers Prestige Books International for bringing out this book so expeditiously and elegantly.

Swarupananda Chatterjee

Introduction

Harold Pinter, the British playwright, has been regarded as one of the most influential dramatists whose writing career spanned more than 50 years. Indeed, he is considered as the foremost representative of British drama in the second half of the 20th century. In 2005, he won the most coveted Nobel Prize in Literature.

Since 1973, Pinter has won recognition as a fighter for human rights and at times as one who took controversial stand on various issues. Like Bernard Shaw, he gave a new direction to English drama. He is admirably considered as the spiritual son of Absurd Theatre and often compared to Samuel Beckett. Pinter is generally called as an existentialist and absurdist playwright as he, in his plays, presents the essential problems of existence: death, alienation, suffering and the inadequacy of language as a means of communication. To portray the sense of absurdity in modern civilized society, Pinter also handles some other crucial issues like identity and politics. The former issues are amply highlighted by the renowned critics. The present study deals with and amplifies the theme of identity and politics in the select works of Harold Pinter. This I am sure will open up a new horizon for the innovative researchers to brood on.

Hence my chief concern is to expose the various aspects of identity and politics involved in Pinter's plays. We get our identity from our positions in society and also from our actions. As our position and actions change in accordance with the situation, we have many identities. Identity basically depends upon the situation and society. Pinter does not overtly address the contemporary fractures in British society but these are clearly seen especially in his early 'room' plays in the form of race, immigration, religion etcetera. Identity is associated closely with them and this type of identity is comprehensible. But there is also another type of identity which comes from the interpersonal relationships and of one's behavior. Pinter as a playwright is more concerned with the individual human behavior than a larger social problem. Most importantly he is very much concerned with how we control our own identities with our use of language. We do it in our life through overtly lying, suppressing information and talking excessively in order to bypass a problem.

In Pinter's drama, the protagonist's sense of identity, his knowing who he is, is disguised in the common thread of his early 'room' plays—the illusion of security. Though in his plays such a sense of security is almost hubristic, yet the world of Pinter does not allow a confident "I am who I am". Thus, Pinter's plays want to establish the truth that no one can have a certain sense of who he is and how he fits into the scheme of things. His plays have the assumption that this central uncertainty controls our existence. Pinter's comedies of menace prove that there can never be any such fixed identity as every attempt to acquire a certain sense of self is destroyed every time.

Identity is presented as fragile throughout Pinter's oeuvre in many different ways. The issues of personal identity are basically exploded by the following apparent categorization: lack of identity, false identity, trading of identity, metamorphosis and breakdown. Some characters in Pinter have no traceable identity (like Riley in *The Room*), they suddenly appear like the strangers. In very few cases, the audience and this type of characters themselves do not know their actual names. The second group of characters can be called 'imposters' because they intentionally misguide those around them and the audience about their true self (like Davies in *The Caretaker*) and sometimes they purposefully accept any identity imposed by others haphazardly. A few strange characters can trade their identity within the short duration of the play (like Ruth in *The Homecoming*). It not only implies the arbitrariness of their characters, but also something more significant. In some cases, the 'victim/victimizer' roles in an individual character have been switched. The ultimate victim of the play, in this metamorphosis, can be found in previous scenes to be victimizing another person (like Stanley in *The Birthday Party*). In the last case, the apparent 'breaking down' of a character's self as well as identity leads to a psychological collapse (Stanley) or sudden physical impairment—generally blindness (Rose). These personal crises in identity actually stand for post-war England's larger social crises. Similarly, the fractured identities of the characters of Pinter's plays are the symbolic representations of the fractured identity of Pinter himself as a London-born Jewish playwright growing up after World War II.

These types of identity are definitely connected with Pinter's another issue, that is, politics. This politics is not the politics of state, nation or political parties but it is the politics of our everyday interpersonal relationships. Politics naturally deals with power, equations, situations, locations and positions. Power politics dealing with the position of individuals in society and in state is largely described by Michel Foucault and Antonio Gramsci. Politics are basically of two kinds. It can be expressed through interpersonal relationships of men and women or through state, government and opposition party activities. This second type of politics features in the conflicts and tensions between parties (Government and Oppositions), ideologies (Capitalism and Socialism, Communalism and Liberalism etcetera), conflicts between groups and communities rather than individuals. Identity may be easily associated with the state or parties, but this is not my concern. My focus is upon the politics of an individual's relationship with others and how it depends on one's identity and also how it subverts one's identity.

These interpersonal power equations basically deal with the questions of dominations, of empowerment and of dispossessions in Pinter's works. Language plays a vital role in this game of identity and politics. In fact, it is language through which identity and politics operate and it is also language through which we can perceive this subtle mechanism. It creates the conditions which are simultaneously meaningless and meaningful. It may be called the postmodern condition.

From this view-point, I shall discuss Pinter's three important plays in the next three chapters. They are *The Homecoming, The Birthday Party* and *The Room.* To penetrate into the deep of the discussion I shall analyze it from theoretical (Literary) perspectives such as post-structuralism, psychoanalysis etcetera.

The Homecoming
A Post-Structural Analysis

In the plays of Harold Pinter, the multiple planes of meaning depend upon cryptic structures of word, thought and action. It is not possible to schematize and reduce these to apt and concrete statements which might directly communicate the variegated responses of readers or spectators. Pinter's fantabulous arrangement of words and gesture, the subtle placing of problematic situations, and combination of the poetic and the conversational rhythms fabricate an intricate texture of suggestions, and encourage diversity of explanation. Peter Hutchinson tried to illuminate this problem by approaching works as such in terms of a game the writer plays with the readers. According to him:

Works which derive their main strength from a single puzzle may (therefore) appear predictable and dull when read a second time. On the other hand, works which rest more on the interaction of enigmatic character, or which present contradictory solutions to fairly complex puzzles, may appear even more compelling and mysterious on renewed contact. (21)

Such an enigma is created by the layers of meaning in *The Homecoming.* They are organized not with just the everyday verbal interaction of the characters of the play but through the violation of naturalism at some strange situation where speeches suddenly slip into the absurd. Yet here the colloquial transaction is subtly stylized and is under poignant control. But as there are multiple levels of meaning, there definitely are the conglomerations of completely different points of view. In doing so Pinter uses language games which have an inherent politics and creates situations which are always controlled by the micro politics of power. This politics can be shown explicitly when the implied suggestion of the complex, fleshy cover of language has been put off.

In *The Homecoming* one cannot find or know the man who is always behind the mask of language. As the plot is not weaved in accordance with the common logic, the mendacity of the characters draws innumerable interpretations. The characters cannot be identified as they are lying and, in that process, they run away from themselves and simultaneously sometimes their identity merges with each other and creates a smokescreen of multiple identities.

The language of *The Homecoming* always plays the game of deception and subterfuge. Like a weapon, here identity is sharpened to attack or barbed round by language and often it is also concealed by that language. To find this weapon, we must have recourse to psychoanalysis of the characters so that we can delve deep into the mind of the characters and can feel the presence of the power structure of the society. The works of some French thinkers might help us in this project—Jacques Lacan, Michel Foucault, Jacque Derrida and Viennese Ludwig Wittgenstein. The clever characters play the language game to obfuscate issues and confuse the less intelligent characters and, in that process, they hide their true intention as well as their true identity and thus project the shadowy and illusory image of themselves. My concern here is to explore the different levels of meaning and to illuminate the true intention and true identity and finally to realize the power politics—social, sexual and familial.

Lucina Paquet Gabbard examines the four plays namely, *The Collection, The Lover*, *Tea Party* and *The Homecoming* as a group of plays dealing with the oedipal wish. It attracts greater critical attention on the linguistic level because of its subterranean interaction of spoken words and inner emotion. It is clearly and significantly evident here that the speeches are mostly used as a cover or hint.

My focus is on *The Homecoming* which is based on a theme of socio-sexual perversion (perversion in terms of the norms of society and Christianity) that is applicable for some characters that do not come from a single office, but they are in reality members of a single family. It is a full length play the beginning of which is in the evening, going through the night and the next morning and finally ending in the afternoon. So, the clock takes a complete circle, similarly the characters meet that point from where their journey starts. It seems as if Pinter has no message to broadcast to the world. Guido Almansi and Simon Henderson rightly comment in the introduction of their book on Harold Printer:

He is an author without authority, a communicator in the paradoxical position of having nothing to say. He is our contemporary in a sense that many of his fellow writers in Britain and British theatre, in particular—are not. For him, as for the post-modernist world generally, it is language that provides the supreme obstacle. He is not part of that fatal tradition in English literature, going back to G.B. Shaw and the theatre of ideas, to D.H. Lawrence and the literature of feelings, according to which language is no problem—the supposed problems being intellection (the manipulation of ideas) and sincerity (the expression of feelings). (11)

In the dream-like structure, the drama explores associated themes of sex and marriage with embedded ambiguities and ambivalence at major points of transition.

In the evening the play begins with the shouting of Max, the father-cum-mother of Lenny and Joey, towards Lenny due to the mere absence of scissors. The lack of response from Lenny irritates him because it also is suggestive of the gradual reduction of the authority of the father in his family. Hence the dethroned father is constantly trying to reassert himself wildly and foolishly also by relating the past incidents where his physical as well as masculine strength was notable. So, he refers to his underworld's life and his heinous friend MacGregor. But the reminiscence of Mac also leads him to his dead wife Jessie. Max here foolishly tries to suppress the fact - the possibility of a clandestine liaison between his wife Jessie and his friend Mac:

> He was very fond of your mother, Mac was. Very fond. He always had a good word for her.
>
> Pause.
>
> Mind you, she wasn't such a bad woman. Even though it made me sick just to look at her rotten stinking face, she wasn't such a bad bitch. I gave her the best bleeding years of my life, anyway. (17).

The word 'such' in 'not such a bad woman' clearly indicates that she was a bad woman but not as such as one can think. The more Max suppresses, the more he expresses. Yet he attempts because that can destroy the illusory pattern of masculinity, he has been building up around himself. Then in a long speech, Max recollects his past in the horse course. It manifests his dormant longing for the phallic strength and also the subjugation of the feminine self. Then comes Sam, Max's brother. Like Max, he brags about himself as a hired—car driver. Here each and everybody is talking about their masculine physical strength. Thus, Pinter establishes subtly the power struggle of the male characters at the very beginning only to be undermined by a female character (Ruth) at the end. But the speeches of Sam, I think, are not unnatural—a man boasting over and over in a humble tone about his professional dexterity is not a sin. We all do it at times. Max is also just like the inner animal of everybody who does not easily accept the supremacy of his junior. He cannot bear with the slow but gradually growing power of his younger family members and sometimes 'gets jealous' (21). Irving Wardle has made an ethnological interpretation of *The Homecoming*: "Pinter used the animal metaphor with discretion encased in a reassuringly human mask. . . all Pinter had done was to remove the mask and show the naked animal. It is a family of predators in which a power contest is going on" (40-44). Max raves at Joey and Sam: "Who do you think I am, your mother. Eh? Honest. They walk in her every time of the day and night like bloody animals. Go and find yourself a mother" (24).

This exposes not only his resentment against the mal-treatment he gets but also the filthy, bestial surrounding. Max calls Sam 'a maggot.' Struggle for power and sexual mastery characterizes what might be called this 'civilized jungle.' Max is a butcher and here he talks of horses too. Lenny says to his father. "Why don't you buy a dog? You're a dog cook. Honest. You think you are cooking for a lot of dogs". (19) Here Lenny also attempts to degrade the position of the father as a cook. Actually, in the absence of their mother Jessie, it is the assault of Lenny on his father's masculinity. With Max and Lenny, the action is set to illuminate "the relationship between power and identity, as characters struggle to gain authority within the family structure. One front of the war is fought among the men, but the key conflict is between these men and the lone woman who invades their home." (Cahn, 55) Here is not only the enigma of identities between man and animal, but also between male and female and such confusion of identity creates an impression of monstrosity. Such almost bestial behavior of the family members violates our sense of rationality.

This unusual relationship within the family fraught with sexual tensions, bewilder the readers. This draws our attention first on Max, who is sexually ambivalent or perhaps—what Lenny says—'sexless.' His constant association with a traditionally female role, notably cooking, clearly makes him a mother-figure. Sometimes he resents this and also sometimes he takes a bitter pride when it suits him—"don't talk to me about the pain of childbirth—I suffered the pain, I've still got the pangs." (55). Simultaneously this man is again aggressively patriarchal, wilding his stick viciously, in the style of his former profession—a typically masculine one—a butcher; but he resents it when Lenny tries to label him as 'Dad.' Even his sincere exposition of his paternal affection towards his eldest son Teddy appears cloyingly maternal in tone—"what about a nice cuddle and kiss, eh?" (51) This is nothing but essentially the hide-and-seek power politics deeply embedded in his voluntarily created identity. Actually, Max willingly enters into the shell of his feminine identity whenever his power game requires and similarly casts it off whenever its requirement is over. In the same way Lenny is also playing his hide-and-seek power game with his Dad. To establish his domination in the family he rebukes badly his old father and even depreciates his cooking also, but as Max is the provider of food in the family, he has to flatter Max extremely and not only that, he also behaves like a kid to Max taking Max as a mother to satisfy his hunger. So, he is also an opportunist as well as a player on the other side of the sea-saw of power politics.

This dual role of Max, both as a patriarchal and matriarchal figure, transparently indicates the archetypal division of labor between the kitchen and the outdoor. This dwindling of sexual identity is also seen in the other members of the family. His brother Sam also has some indication of Max's ambivalence. According to Richard Dutton, "he is apparently homosexual" (126) ("any one could have you at the same time. You'd bend over for half a dollar on Blackfriars Bridge", 56). It presumably justifies his pointedly a-sexual memories of Jessie: "Used to just drive her about. It was my pleasure." (24) His speech about "getting a bit peckish" points not only to himself physically as a hungry and irritated man but also to the state of the family and his place in it as the family itself is hungry for a renovation in its power structure. Sam is no longer compatible enough to cope with the other dominant males in the game of "take the piss". Sam is "a childless bachelor, outside the squabble for social dominance. In social units throughout the animal kingdom, a male who does not father offspring forfeits his most fundamental masculine prerogative, and such creatures are outcasts. So too, is Sam mocked by the others for his noncombatant status." (Cahn, 57) But being a character of least sexual energy, he also confuses us when his brother pokes him by telling him unmarried in spite of being a good chauffeur and 'a man with all your gifts' (22). He replies that 'there is still time' to marry. It also clearly denotes his psychosexual virility and his longing for a perfect bride.

Few hours later at night the light of the play falls on Teddy, Max's eldest son and his wife Ruth standing on the threshold of Teddy's paternal house. Teddy and his wife Ruth had been visiting Italy, and on their way back, it seems as if Teddy had decided to visit the house where he was born and to introduce Ruth to his family whom she has never met before. But from here the questions start peeping in the mind. Why does Teddy not want to wake anyone of his family? Instead, he wants Ruth to come up to bed with him, as his old room is still empty there. It may be that Teddy does not want to introduce Ruth to his family, but Ruth's insistence may compel him to do so. Teddy is completely aware of the sexual hunger of his family members. So, it is natural for him to keep Ruth on his own protection. Being a professor of Philosophy at a college in America, he cannot say it to his wife because his sense of self-respect and his superior position in their conjugal hierarchy prevent him from discussing it with his wife about it. The past of Ruth as a nude model always places Teddy in a higher position in this game of power, so he should not expose his weakness to his wife. So, the knowledge of the past is also the source of power in such a little familial politics. But here we can also find another level of meaning. Teddy's marriage to Ruth may be on the verge of breakdown and hence this is a very authentic motivation for the sudden and unplanned tour to Venice. It is just like the last-minute attempt at a second honeymoon to save their conjugal life and maybe it is Ruth's last attempt to know something about Teddy which would help her to bring up their children. But the probability is that their tour cannot give birth to the desired result and that is why Ruth refuses to go up to Teddy's bedroom on her first arrival in her in-law house. Her reluctance naturally is the outcome of an unsatisfactory or monotonous sexual relationship.

Teddy's next brother who has not been able to sleep now happens to meet Teddy. The meeting of the two brothers after a long period of six years is strangely very casual. Teddy then goes into his own room while Lenny sits downstairs, smoking. Ruth comes back and meets with Lenny. Lenny finds his equivalent when faced with Ruth. They both are good players of language games and both love to be in the make-believe world. For example, I think, they together dream of the Italian military campaign. But in their first encounter of imagination Ruth plausibly gives us the sign of her being a better player. Lenny wishes: "If I'd been a soldier in the last war—say in the Italian campaign—I'd probably found myself in Venice" (38). Ruth, in a different context, says, "But if I would have been a nurse in the Italian campaign I would have been there before" (63). Reality controls our language, but in their world, language controls reality. As in fantasizing, Ruth surpasses Lenny; similarly, Ruth has better control over language than Lenny. Lenny attempts to conquer Ruth by verbal stratagem. He first proposes her 'refreshment of some kind.' But after she denies his overture, he insults her by telling her that they do not have an alcoholic drink in the house. Ruth does not respond to his insult or to his verbal attack. But now she is just under the process of making herself aware of Lenny's technique. Then Lenny uses the same tactic in another way. He asks her about the connection of her with his brother and when Ruth replies to him, "I am his wife" (36), he immediately changes the topic. This switching is actually the exposition of ignorance and a direct insult to overpower her. It is a battle of wills in the ground of language and here we must remember the Viennese philosopher Wittgenstein who in his famous book *Philosophical Investigation* showed that human relationships are of a practical and finite nature. They are lived and experienced, and need acknowledgement rather than justification and proof. It is a struggle for domination, on which now Lenny is in a higher position. Lenny now takes advantage of Ruth's coming at night. He does not hesitate to get a minimal chance of attacking Ruth in a roundabout way: "There are lots of things which tick in the night, don't you find that? All sorts of objects, which, in the day, you wouldn't call anything else but commonplace. They give you no trouble. But in the night any given one of a number of them is liable to start letting out a bit of a tick whereas you look at these objects in the day and they're just commonplace. They're as quiet as mice during the daytime." (36)

Apparently, it is the clock which disturbs his sleeping, but if you go deep into it, you will find another meaning. Ruth as an outsider in the daytime may be Teddy's wife, but at the middle of the night she might be something dirty, something affronting. Ruth remains silent like before about it. She even does not react to his further assault - sexual provocation, which defames her status as his elder brother's wife: "Isn't it funny? I've got my pyjamas on and you're fully dressed" (37). Lenny, being inspired by her silence, continues taunting her. His behavior implies that Ruth may have left her husband as Lenny feigns shock on Ruth's reply "we are on a visit to Europe" (37) and ridicules her morality "what, both of you?" His malicious style reflects as if he is speaking with his brother's illegal mistress. So, he asks her mockingly, "what, you sort of live with him over there, do you?". This entire he has done only to capture her mind in the net of her powerful language. He, I think, wants to insinuate the idea that in Europe Ruth may see nothing but the bedroom walls as he states, "on a visit to Europe, eh? Seen much of it?" (37) In this context we should remember Guido Almansi and Simon Henderson's writing:

> The battles remain constrained at a purely verbal level, actual violence being only hinted at in Lenny's threatening speeches and resorted to in moments of sheer desperation by the weakest of the foursome, Max. to resort to violence is to acknowledge defeat, for *The Homecoming* is essentially a play about language—about articulating a language and being articulated by a language. In Pinter's world social control lies ultimately in the power to impose one's language on another. Hitler knew this well: if you succeed in putting the words

> Ubermensch and Herrenvolk into other people's mouths, then your battle is already won. (61)

So, it is very difficult to say who the winner of this language game is. From now we can see the effect of Lenny's verbal attack on Ruth. Is she subdued or not? Lenny himself wants to examine it. Ruth does not reply to the underlying derision of Lenny's words, she only reacts to the surface words. When Lenny wants permission twice from her to hold her hand, she in both cases denies and asks him why. One can say it is her not raffling due to Lenny's threat and hence Lenny begins to get what he wants. But on the other hand, it may be also said that it is Ruth's challenge: it is the first place where she more subtly denies him satisfaction and control. Almansi and Henderson call Lenny 'a supreme conversationalist,' 'an anti-plagiarist.' (63) The plagiarist usurps and uses other's language as his own, but the anti-plagiarist puts his own language forcefully like Hitler on other's mouth. From their viewpoint, "Lenny like Mick in The Caretaker aspires to be an anti-plagiarist by setting the tone, style and subject matter of the conversation. He wants to be able to select the entire grammar and vocabulary of every verbal exchange." (63) So, he threatens her by telling two stories about hitting and kicking a syphilitic woman and an old woman. Maybe she has been threatened or shocked, so she does not want to show it but she feigns taking it lightly and intimates disconcertingly by asking "how did you know she was diseased". To it Lenny replies, "How did I know? (Pause) I decided she was." (39) In this context it becomes to Almansi the equivalent of 'I said she was.' It is the linguistic threat, not physical. Instead of gagging people, Lenny un-gags them, like Iago in *Othello* he very artistically insinuates a way into the dark, deep, psychic strong- hold of their language.

Apart from this view of Almansi and Henderson, we can see it from different perspectives. Ruth's question to Lenny does not come from fear but more subtly it shows that violence of this story, Lenny wants to assert, does not concern her. It is the first counter–

attack and it is the first place where Ruth's female power is established with full assertiveness. So now the riddle is that no one finds the true winner in this situation still now. Who is the supreme ventriloquist? In this regard, I have to illuminate why Lenny, all of a sudden, starts telling about his hooliganism. It is Ruth whose indifference towards Lenny's verbal fisticuffs makes Lenny cast off his slough of feinting attack and compels him to direct attack. Simon Trussler opines: Ruth forces him into long, rambling anecdotes which put off the moment. When a gesture must be made, a gambit followed through: and so, Lenny launches into a long story about a girl who began 'taking liberties with me,' but who was 'falling apart with the pox,' and next into a tale about and old lady who wanted his help moving a mangle. Both anecdotes end in acts of violence—towards, that is, the whore of the first story, and the mother-figure of the second (123). Thus, from Trussler's article we get the glimpse of the dramatist's skill as Ruth will have the identity of both the whore and a mother-figure.

In the final scene of this verbal fighting, we see them bullying a glass of water that, unasked, Lenny gave her to drink. Now she refuses to return it. Their struggling for the glass is symbolic for their struggling for domination—symbolic in the sense that both of their words are always trying to frame a possibility, a conception, rather than reality. It may be wholly suggestive of reality. In this context we should remember the article of Bert O. States where he writes: "Lenny accomplishes this by satirizing his act in the language his 'betters' habitually use to sanitize themselves from dockside realities of just this short. The effect, of course, is to make him superior to his brutality, to the class morality he is mimicking, and to his freshest opponent in what his soul brother Mick, in The Caretaker, calls 'the game.' . . . Life is all performance for Lenny, a veritable charade of politesse." (Bloom 15)

But apart from this framing of conception, Martin Esslin pigeon-holes Pinter by declaring, "Ruth has won the contest of wills". (130) I am completely reluctant to agree with him as he, in his book *Pinter the Playwright*, doggedly attributes certain confined meanings to the playwright. Finally, when Lenny threatens Ruth to take the glass, instead of getting feared, Ruth reasserts her power by threatening to take him.

This fight for possession of tongue is in the realm of private language (which Wittgenstein repudiates in the *Investigations*) and it is opposite to the fight for the possession of soul. In this realm of language, behind the surface there are ideas, emotions, feelings and amorous or sexual longings. Common people struggle against all odds to be 'a bit inner,' but Pinter is the only writer who has transformed psychological depth and inwardness into an insult. Following Wittgenstein, Pinter sees that we are the prisoners of the delusive power of language. This brought him close to Wittgenstenian philosophy—the shaming power of the word can simulate real things so well that no discriminating power of the word allows us to distinguish lies from truth. It can deceive us in the very act of singling us out as those to whom truth is delivered. It is the knowledge, as far as I think, which makes the words deceptive. For example, in *The Homecoming*, we now see some events which have a greater impact on our mind. Earlier he told her not to call him Leonard because it is the name his mother gave him. This clearly implies that Lenny now begins to see his mother's shadow in her and he tries ardently to prevent it. So, his prohibition to Ruth implies that she is not good enough to call him by this name. Now my question is which factor or which 'knowingness' about Ruth causes him to do so. To find its answer I have to do an amateur psychoanalysis. Prior to this event, Lenny's avoidance of Ruth's identifying herself as Teddy's wife comes from his unconscious. It might happen that the family long before had got some information about Teddy's marriage with a nude model—hence a near prostitute. This floating news might have gone to the deep of forgotfulness or has been repressed into the unconscious. His avoidance, his prohibition may be the production of his unconscious. Lacan in his essay 'The Subversion of the

Subject and the Dialectic of Desire in The Freudian Unconscious' says, "L'inconscient est discours de l' Autre" ("desire becomes bound up at the junction with the Other's desire"; Lacan 679), that is, unconscious consists of other's discourse.

The other evidence of this may be Max's insulting her as a tart, a slut, a scrubber, a whore, a slop bucket, a bedpan and a disease on his first meeting, without any reason. Above all these, Max's tongue has slipped from the unconscious, "I've never had a whore under this roof before. Ever since your mother died." (50). I think it comes off also from Max's unconscious like Lenny and it is the knowledge about Ruth got from others which causes it. Lacan firmly believes that unconscious is also structured by language and unconscious has no existence beyond the realm of language. So, the first rejection of Ruth by the family is hardly tangible to us as it is the language of the unconscious. Now being an amateur psychoanalyst, I must discuss Freud and Lacan. Being influenced by Claude Levi-Strauss's *Les Structures e de la Parente,* Lacan in the second part of his essay 'The Function and Field of Speech and Language in Psychoanalysis,' explains that in any society the organization of a family is basically constituted by barter of women and as soon as the family organized, a deep sense of relation is simultaneously constructed and in its deepest core language and unconscious are very active to prevent the incestuous desire. In this family of the play the mother died long before. Now a mother like figure, wife of the elder brother—substitute of the father—has come. So, the long repressed incestuous desire of the family members surges up. So, Lenny's mind has now become extremely turbulent when Ruth demeaningly puts him in the position of a child, inviting him to sit on her lap while he sips, then while she pours water into his mouth. This mother-like stance of Ruth draws an image of his mother in Lenny's unconscious all of a sudden. But giving him no time to adjust with this situation suddenly Ruth commands him to lie on the floor and transforms her image to a whore by proposing to pour it down his throat. This vexes Lenny's mind from unconscious to conscious. Her presence has threatened the individual identity of every other member. There is fine dramatic irony when Ruth says, "I am not making any noise" and Teddy promptly agrees: "I know you are not" (31). Her presence indeed creates a stir in the stationary waterfront of this North London family. Lenny comments later: "then you come here . . . and start to make trouble" (42). Ruth symbolizes the turning point in the family setup. Ruth laughs, drinks the water, smiles and leaves. Lenny's puzzled, defeated mind cannot help shouting behind her. Here I must mention Freud's famous essay 'The Dissolution of the Oedipus Complex.' At the centre of Freud's theory of childhood development is the Oedipus complex. According to Freud, a boy's close relation to his mother, as the primary love object leads to a desire for complete union with her. A girl, on the other hand, who is similarly attached to the mother and thus caught up in a homosexual desire, directs her libido (love, sexual energy broadly construed) towards her father (often called 'Electra complex'). This produces a triadic relationship regardless of one's sex, with the parent of the same sex cast in the role of a rival for the affection of the parent of the opposite sex. The boy will eventually abandon his incestuous desire for his mother out of fear of being castrated by his father. This fear arises when the boy comes to realize that females are castrated and imagines that he may be also a victim if he does not subordinate his desire for the mother. Thus, the boy represses his incestuous desire in his latency period, adjusts to the reality principal and waits for the day when he will be the patriarch. In this way the boy identifies with his father and the symbolic role of manhood.

In *The Homecoming*, the sons Lenny and Joey completely suffer from the Oedipus complex. Max, the family's father oscillated between his external and home life, having failed to strike a bargain between the two. "I should have been a trainer. Many times I was offered the job . . . but I had family obligations, my family needed me at home" (18). The question arises as to what type of need this had been. Had it been that Jessie had no time for the family, for looking after the kids and home? If so, why is it so? Pradip Lahiri, in his book *Harold Pinter: A Study in Dialogic Art*, tries to find the answer: "*The Homecoming* through its dialogue continues to raise doubt about Jessie's role and her character. Max's words have very clear implications that his wife's domestic role and performance had been far from adequate, and that Max had to fill the vacuum of her domestic duties for most of his life. His words are "I gave her the best bleeding years of my life, anyway." 'anyway' has a string of implications attached to it, for in Pinter's drama no word is used without an import." (93)

So, it is clear that the sons did not get their mother adequately in their child age and naturally it would create a strong desire, whether you may say it psychosexual towards their mother. So, the whole drama is plunged into the oedipal complex as we now see in the second act of the play how "fantasy overpowers rationality in the Freudian psychoanalysis when a woman arrives in a sex starved male orbit". (Lahiri 89)

This other wave of meaning found in the psychoanalysis of the play is also plunged in politics. It is the subtle politics of the language to puzzle the audience into the mystery of the dream. The whole drama *The Homecoming* may be thought of as a dream as the homecoming of the couple happens at night. To a social law-abiding man who strictly follows each and every norm of society, it is nothing but a gibberish nightmare, but to a sensitive man it is nothing but a broken mirror whose every reflection has a glimpse of our idiosyncrasies. So, this work may be, to some extent, regarded as a Dream—work, as the Dream-work is the production of dreams during sleep—the translation of demands arising from the unconscious into the symbolic object of the preconscious and eventually the conscious mind of the subject.

To establish the logic of this oedipal complex we need some justifications which we can find in Freud's another book *Totem and Taboo* where he gives some notion about this happened in the ancient days of civilization. There was a time when each female member of the family was fit to be possessed by the chief of the family - that is the father. But the son had not any such right and hence one day the sons tried to kill their father in order to usurp the paternal right to incest. But a strong sense of remorse and sin began to undermine them after the parricide and from that time they themselves decided that the females would be no longer the commodity of their making sex. According to Freud, this is the origin of the incest taboo. But this repressed desire of incest sometimes haunts the individual and here in this drama especially in its second act we find the son's eagerness to do so and to defeat their father.

The psychological complexity has its seed in the beginning of the first act where Max says to Lenny "what have you done with Scissors?". Followed by a pause, it continues "I said I am looking for the scissors. What have you done with them?". Now comes another pause and again he says "Did you hear me? I want to cut something out of the paper." Then his son Lenny replies with, "I am reading the paper". (15) The play opens with thirty-seven words, three questions and three pauses, simply presenting the unusual, vicious and violent conflict between the father and the son. The father can cut, destroy and even kill; hence the two words 'scissors' and 'something' are clearly resonant of the castration—the father's threat with it and then the son's rejection of it and son's counter attack - 'hit below the belt.'

Now what is the point in the brawl between Lenny and Max whereas Max is so careful about Joey's boxing and not only that, he constantly begs affection from his elder son Teddy. So, the negligence of his son Lenny by his father raises the problem of fatherhood and it culminates when Sam—'the family's conscience, its super-ego' (Esslin 145) reveals the secret that Max's closest friend, terror of the west end, MacGregor "had Jessie in the back of my cab as I drove them along" (86). Hence who is the bastard of the three fine grown-up lads? Is it Lenny? Lenny is skeptic about his paternal identity, so he dares to tease his legal, social father: "That night . . . you know . . . the night you got me . . . the night with Mum, what was it like? Eh? When I was just a glint in your eye. What is it like? What was the background to it? I mean, I want to know the real facts about my background. [. . .] It's a question long overdue, from my point of view, but as we happen to be passing the time of day here tonight I thought I'd pop it to you." (44)

It is a question that many of us never had the courage to ask. It also puts Max in a crisis of identity as what the legal father is doing when the biological process of the production of his son is going on by his wife with probably his best friends. Max replies savagely "you'd drown in your own blood" (44). It is clearly an indication of his present anger and past jealousy. From the book *Harold Pinter* by William Baker some information about this line has been derived: "There is manuscript evidence revealing that Pinter repressed much more than actually appears in the script. At this point, he first typed 'stuff your face into glass' and then 'stuff your face with broken glass.' This was subsequently changed to 'shove it into a blade of glass' and then 'drown in your own bastard blood.' The viciousness here and the violence is even more overt than in the final dramatic text with the characters going for the jugular or the psychological weak points that they can detect in one another." (65)

This heinous violence can be contrasted clearly to his affectionate—'but you are my own flesh and blood' (57) to Teddy. On the other hand, this drowning in blood may be interpreted as wishful thinking: the bastard son deserves to be condemned as an aborted foetus which drowns in the mother's menstrual blood. After such stormy violence Lenny remains apparently imperturbable as ever. He again contemplates and whispers: "I should have asked my dear mother. Why didn't I ask my dear mother?" (45) In this scene the play resembles Strindberg's *Storm Weather* (*Ovader)* which has the hints but never the affirmation of whether the prematurely senile protagonist is the legitimate father of the child. But there is also another mode of interpretation of this situation as Lenny's line of inquiry and his consequent calmness is also indicative of his 'knowingness' like Oedipus's.

Sophocles' play *Oedipus Tyrannus* on which Freud works is about the dangers and complexities of knowingness. The name Oedipus in Greek has resonances of 'swollen footed' and 'to know': he is weak footed but strong minded. Throughout the play, his 'knowingness' is emphasized. He becomes the tyrant of Thebes because of his cleverness rather than who he is. He solves the riddle of Sphinx, and she goes and kills herself, but wreaks the terrible vengeance of the plague on Thebes. Oedipus does not kill her himself as the usual hero does. Oedipus continually jumps to conclusions, as though too anxious to grasp the full meaning of what he is doing. He assumes meaning is transparent to human reason and that he knows what the problem is. He has been told that he will kill his father and marry his mother, yet he quickly kills a man old enough to be his father and marries a woman old enough to be his mother—and is proud of it! On hearing an oracle—notorious for their ambiguity—he immediately assumes he knows what it means. Sophocles is giving a critique of knowingness. Oedipus was abandoned by his parents and in response abandoned himself to knowing. Similarly, Lenny is abandoned by his mother for her premature death and by his biological father and also to some extent by his legitimate, social father. His problem is due to his suspicion and knowingness. Lenny, like Oedipus, also glorifies the powers of his mind, as it is too painful to recognize his loss. He acts out his abandonment.

This Oedipal complex may make him speak in such a way. It cannot be said that in the course of his thinking of his mother's nuptial bed, the nude figure of his mother does not float in his own mind for a single moment and his repressed desire to replace his father-figure comes true when a mother like figure of his family has come to his arms. This is a wish fulfillment dream-work to the sons. The very ease with which Ruth is persuaded to accept the profession of part-time prostitution and to become a readily available sexual partner for Lenny and Joey seems completely a dream of night in which wishes miraculously come true. So, the homecoming part of the drama may be a dream because the way in which Lenny meets with Ruth suddenly in the middle of a night when she has appeared ghostly from nowhere supports all the traits of the manner in which dreams develop from a subconscious of lying in bed and imagining what one would most desire to happen. According to Lacan, it is neurosis. Freud and Lacan both talked about two mental conditions—foreclosure and repression—which are characteristically opposite. The insatiable desire of an individual which has been repressed without any transformation to the unconscious by the super–ego becomes latent and in the crucial situations of life this repressed desire rises up: it is neurosis. The three sons' carnal desire for their mother in their unconsciousness rises up when Ruth comes but it is difficult to interpret it for Teddy. Marc Silverstein says in his book *Harold Pinter and the Language of Cultural Power*: "While the play clearly manifests Oedipal tensions, I would argue that these tensions indicate a scenario more Lacanian than Freudian. Lacan's conceptualization of the Oedipus complex emphasizes the family's status as a network of symbolic relations that must generate appropriate subjects to occupy the positions these relations designate, and thus provides a useful theoretical lens through which to view *The Homecoming*. The complexities of the Lacanian Oedipal scenario demand an excursus into the realm of theory that, while somewhat lengthy, will help clarify Jessie's role in the crisis of family structure Pinter dramatizes."

For Lacan, "father" and "mother" are signifying spaces, symbolic positions that function as linguistic categories, drawing their meaning from the play of difference that defines their relationship within the closed signifying system formed by the family. The mother's recognition of the father's word promotes the elaboration of difference within the family. Recognizing the father's discursive power, the mother proclaims her own inadequacy—her "lack" thus defines his "potency," and his "potency" constitutes both her necessary "lack" and her desire for plenitude that will complete it. (88-89)

The non-realism of Pinter's stage has set the scene for a ritual. In this ritual a family full of psychically depleted men derives power (or in Sam and Max's case, wither away) with a surrogate mother-figure - Ruth who through her own ritualized initiation into the role of the goddess achieves her signified potency as the ancient archetype of Lilith. Silverstein proclaims that every family has its own subconscious construct of the Lacanian Oedipal drives. He also asserts that these natural drives are perfectly illustrated in each character and their relationships to women. Here, the subconscious is tangible in Pinter's stage-reality and characters, and it drives the play's heightened realism that borders on the surreal. The absent character or the delegated sensibility of this drama is Jessie, who defines herself and her overbearing presence in Max's dominating discourse. Here Ruth embodies Jessie and Teddy becomes a composite of all the other male characters in the play, each signifying a different element of the male consciousness.

But Teddy may also be considered as a defeated Oedipus to his father where Max is the victor. It is just as possible, for that particular case, to fit this eldest son into the pattern of the play by thinking of him as a sort of modern Oedipus, who has been sleeping with his mother-substitute in his ignorance but loses her to the father he has not got the guts to kill. Bert O. States in this regard gives us some important information:

A New York psychoanalyst has suggested the Teddy is an example of a 'totally withdrawn libido' troubled by a basic hatred for women and a tendency towards homosexuality (a family problem); he therefore substitutes intellectual equilibrium for a proper sex life. Michael Craig, who played Teddy, says he is the most violent of all the brothers, a veritable "Eichmann" underneath who has "Rationalized his aggressions". Pinter, with characteristic simplicity (if not pure disinterest), says he walks out in the end to avoid a "messy fight", and anyway his marriage was on the rocks. All of these ideals do not arise from the speech alone, of course, but the speech authorizes them; it puts the lid, so to speak, on Teddy's possibilities. (Bloom 8)

But Max, the father of the family, is seen defeated from the other two sons' point of view. Here Lenny's oedipal wish may be celebrated as pointed by Martin Esslin: "The final image of *The Homecoming* therefore is the culmination of their oedipal dreams; their mother, young and beautiful, has become available to them as a sexual partner, as a 'whore,' while the defeated father grovels on the floor pleading for some scraps of her sexual favors. This wish—fulfillment dream is the exact reversal of the real situation that faces a young son: the father in proud possession and the son rejected, oppressed, dominated." (143)

From the psychosexual interpretation of the play, we should draw our attention to the restrictive ethnic framework though Pinter never shows it explicitly. After watching Teddy and Ruth, Max tells his elder son, "Listen, you think I don't know why you didn't tell me you are married? I know why." (67) Max's explanation of it is couched in general terms and reflects the ethnic differences: "you were ashamed. You thought I'd be annoyed because you married a woman beneath you. You should have known me better. I'm broad minded. I'm a broad-minded man" (67). By this broad-mindedness he actually suggests himself that he is above all these ethnic differences. This game would be clear if we attend to the nuances of the names in the play. The name Max, Sam, Joey and Lenny are common names in the Jewish families of London. So, it is the Jewish blood through Teddy, who has left his family in his early age, has his name's connection almost towards Anglo—Saxon. According to this, the names of Ruth and Jessie are particularly connected. In the Old Testament, Ruth, a Moabite woman—when her first Jewish husband died—went to the land of Judah in Palestine. She lived in that alien land in the house of her mother-in-law Naomi and gleaned corns in the fields of Boaz, a kinsman of her mother-in-law. Eventually she was married again to her kinsman and so became the great—grandmother of King David and hence ancestor of Christ. Her grandson, the father of David, was Jesse, from whose tree the descent of Christ is usually drawn. This association would turn up far—fetched if we do not look at Pinter's childhood friend Morris Wernick's father—a London taxi driver who has some resemblance with Max, a chauffeur. Actually, Morris Wernick wrote many years later, "I married in 1956 and left immediately to start life in Canada. I never told my father that I was married [to a non-Jew] and for the" following near about ten years, "continued to keep up this pretence even on my infrequent visits to England". (Supple 163-64). In 1964, he brought his wife and children to meet his father for the first time. Reflecting in the early years of the twenty first Century, Wernick who spent his career as a university professor of English in Canada observes "forty years ago marrying out was still not regarded lightly" (Supple 163-64). Tremendous psychological pressure was put upon the sons by the parental figures to marry the right girl. From here we can draw the logic of why Teddy has the right key to his home after such a long time. Here I am, to some extent, agree with Barry Supple's remark that *The Homecoming* "drawing more explicitly than Pinter's other plays on the social and cultural problems of his generation, is essentially a play about intermarriage . . . the interaction between the family and the Gentile intruder, the basic clash of social facts and sexual tensions, create a framework within which the place otherwise nightmarish ending assumes at least the semblance of meaning." (7, 31) I disagree with his last words. Pinter in his play *The Homecoming* does not establish any fixed meaning. One cannot be determined with the play's message. For an example, if one says that it is a feminist play, the other critical opinion certainly will raise about its misogyny.

From the misogynist perspective, the drama deals with the horrors of femalehood taking its inspiration from Strindberg who seems to have influenced Pinter. Every character of the play hated women in their own way, though the author remains neutral. Max is haunted by the memory of his 'slut bitch' wife and rebukes the new female visitor as a 'dirty tart,' 'smelly scrubber,' 'slag' and 'tit.' Mark Betty in this respect rightly comments, "These words in themselves are not only demeaning of women; they also actuate a further abasement of women in Max's application of them to slur the male members of his family. As well as firmly establishing the misogynistic tone, such vocabulary is also typical of the linguistic distancing that the characters place between their words and their emotional being." (40)

In the case of the sons, Lenny's profession drives him to psychological as well as physical exploitation, and to threat against women. The moronic Joey screws mechanically, as if making love is just another 'demolition job' and knows only his own physical satisfaction while not knowing how to satisfy the female partner. Teddy treats his wife nothing but a less than precious commodity, understanding neither her needs nor her point of view just like Joey. So, he asks his wife "why do you want a breath of air" (32). So, the male members of the family do not require a caring woman in their house but a sexually 'sympathetic woman' (59) who would be ready to kiss, to be screwed, to be wide open and to deliver the gravy.

Now considered from the feminist angle, the play is the battle field of the heroine where she is the victor of the game. Ruth abandons her husband to gain her freedom from the golden cage of a professor's wife on whom sex has no hold, whose post-doctoral demands require only a bourgeois wife or Ibsenesque 'doll.' The way she speaks so simply yet so movingly of the rock, sand and insects in America illustrates this. Used by men all her life (by photographers who sold pictures of her body; and by Teddy who took her to America) Ruth finally uses her body to break the stereotypes set by the male. When she hears Max, Lenny and Joey discussing putting her on the streets as though she is someone to be manipulated, she is not outraged but demands the best deal for herself. By using her sexuality—her most potent weapon—she establishes authority over the men. John Jenkins rightly comments, "The men who had naturally thought they would dominate her find themselves dominated by her. It is not a question of morality, but of survival; not of justice but of power". (114) Ruth achieves her freedom just as Sarah Woodruff gains her heroic independence in John Fowles's novel *The French Lieutenant's Woman*—by 'marrying Shame' (a key phrase in Fowles's novel). Sarah becomes independent as a woman and gets freed from the manacles of her institutionalized role as governess by accepting to be in popular imagination the French Lieutenant's whore and in real life Charles's mistress for a single night. Similarly, Ruth, by agreeing to satisfy the household's sexual hunger and by becoming a whore, also gets paradoxically liberated from the academic uniform of the philosopher's lowly wife to the fetterless intoxication of the flesh. So, the play is clearly imbued with the plea of feminism as famous critic of Pinter—Michael Billington, who interprets the play "as a feminist challenge to male despotism and to the classification of women as either mothers or whores", identifies the "elusive Ruth" as "escaping from an arid marriage and a sterile academic environment into one where she exercises social, sexual and economic control" (168).

But from this dual mode of the play comes another question—then who is the victor of the whole game of power. Till now Lenny, Ruth, Joey and Max all fulfills the wish to some extent, but it is Teddy who apparently seems the household's sole victim. But if we look at it from the opposite point of view of a frustrated and vindictive husband, then the drama will have the supreme victor named Teddy. The drama shows us that before introducing his family to Ruth, Teddy describes his father to her: "I think you'll like him very much. Honestly". But from what we have seen till now in the drama, his statement is completely a lie and the word 'honestly' designed to reassure her, has a disconcerting effect on us, implying that he willingly misguides her. This misleading intensifies when he further describes his family as "very warm people, really. Very warm. They're my family. They're not ogres" (31). This speech cannot be technically called lie because it has an ambiguous tone. Warm means both loveable and passionate or heated (as they are in their hostilities), but it is certain that Teddy misleads her because his 'very warm' and the adverb 'really' are clearly over acting. From the remaining part of the play Ruth would learn whether the members of the family are ogres or not. From this deviousness we now realize the politics of Teddy who very calmly and cleverly takes his revenge upon his dirty family and his dirty wife. He did not introduce Ruth to his affectionate father or the not ogre's family not only before his marriage but till six years after his marriage. Teddy did not do so then but he does it now because probably he expects to happen later what he expected to happen then. Another plausible reason is that Teddy may have listened to the whispering of his friends and familiars about Ruth's past life behind his back which crosses the limits of his tolerance. So, he makes a scheme to leave Ruth to her past life and does not give Ruth a chance to get a whiff of his plan. This logic, in fact, underlies Pinter's statement to John Lahr that if ever there was a villain in the play, Teddy was it. To conclude with the same opinion of Peter Hall (Lahr 20) and Paul Rogers (Lahr 169) we must say, "Teddy is the biggest bastard of the lot".

There is another controversy about the title of the play: whose homecoming is it. In the first act, Teddy says, "I was born here" (30) to Ruth. So, it is his returning to his own paternal home. But when Teddy gives her the key for her nocturnal walk, he gives her the possession of his home. Homecoming does not mean a mere coming back to house but also to a state of being, a set of relationships, attitudes and values. In this respect it is the homecoming of Ruth as she swings back to her past life—seller of body and it is clearly indicative in the second act by her speech "I was born quite near here" (61). It also may be the homecoming of all as they have all come home to what they want—Joey has a mother, Max has a wife and Lenny has a whore.

Regression can also be seen in the backward movement through the developmental phases of life. The movement of the play actually begins with the return of repressed wishes—Oedipal wishes. All these returning wishes are also homecomings. Ruth's repressed eroticism returns along with the old wish to take the mother's place. The family's repressed desires for mother return and take the form of a need to possess and debase her. (Gabbard 195-96)

All of their wish fulfillment regarding to their sexual instinct if is driven by 'Eros' (called by the Greek) which gives a heavy energy to the birth and living of various species in this world, then another instinct would be equally active in this terrestrial existence—Death instinct which is called 'Thanatos' also by the Greek. In the play we find calmness come into the stage after the satisfaction of desire. Sigmund Freud in his *Beyond the Pleasure Principle* tries to prove by the contemporary biological discoveries that as the birth of life happens in an inanimate condition in the mother's womb, so every living being in its unconscious is always eager to return to that lifeless condition. This has been called by Freud Death-instinct: "Those instincts are therefore bound to give a deceptive appearance of being forces tending towards change and progress, whilst in fact they are merely seeking to reach an ancient goal by paths alike old and new . . . we shall be compelled to say that the aim of all life is death and, looking backwards, that inanimate things existed before living ones." (310-11).

In this play the death of Jessie pervades. Teddy with his 'intellectual equilibrium' (70) maintains the detachment from this mundane world. So, he comes from the darkness and now would go into the darkness. He takes life as an object of observation. Other members of his family cannot think about it; they themselves are objects. So only Teddy can realize this Death–instinct and to some extent—Sam. To Heidegger, death is the only thing of one's own with which the others have no connection. There is no relation of inter subjectivity with death. In literature there are plenty of examples of such attraction of death—attraction of darkness, of infirmity. Famous Bengali poet Jibanananda Das in his poem 'Darkness' (Andhakar) wrote "I have wished to lie merged like eternal death in the bosom and the womb of darkness" (translated by Indrani Halder in *A Certain Sense Poems by Jibanananda Das,* 30). The first word of Pinter's other drama *Old Times* is 'dark.' This inclination towards the darkness, towards mother's womb is symbolically presented by Sam's probable death, though it is a far-fetched comparison.

However, in this play's constantly vicious struggles of power, we can say no character is clearly victorious or all character is victorious. And in doing so, we can reach a decision that in this drama Pinter leaves no situation which has a monolithic, determinate, rigid meaning. Each moment has not only a singular or a double meaning, but it is the rain of meanings. Each interpretation has different politics of its own and different power play in this marginal family of the society. Here power has not any single centre, but it has a multidimensional field to operate. So obviously the question will arise that who is the gainer of this exercise of power or whose power is this. In this drama we transparently see that every character has its own will to dominate or to overpower whether he or she is powerful or powerless. So here power is completely decentred. Here Pinter is completely Foucauldian: "It is a machine in which everyone is caught, those who exercise power just as much as those over whom it is exercised. This seems to me to be the characteristic of the societies installed in the nineteenth century. Power is no longer substantially identified with an individual who possesses or exercises it by right of birth; it becomes machinery that no one owns. Certainly, everyone does not occupy the same position; certain positions preponderate and permit an effect of supremacy to be produced. This is so much the case that class domination can be exercised just to the extent that power is dissociated from individual might." (Foucault 156)

Thus, the characters in the play have not any single, rigid identity also because in this power- merry- go-round their position momentarily changed so everyone in the play is simultaneously victor and victim, gainer and loser. No clear vision of any character we get from the drama as in our real life we just pretend to have known all the wills of our near and dear ones. The more we want to know the more we enter the 'dark continent' of the mind. In this sense most enigmatic is Ruth—her character can be interpreted in thousands of ways just like Mona Lisa or a modern Iphigenia. About her Bill Naismith is absolutely precise: "From a symbolic or mythological viewpoint she has been seen as a fertility goddess, bringing new life and redemption to a barren landscape. From a psychoanalytical view-point she, as a woman, fulfills the subconscious or dream-wishes of the males of the family. From a sociological view—point she is the victor in a struggle for territory: she has taken over the room." (147) So, the analysis of the play is clearly running through the deconstruction to the post–modernism as it embodies the game of rule breaking, the game of iconoclasm.

The play subverts the general notion. Like a pastiche it, to some extent, pieces together incongruous elements and forms from a number of existing genres and finally subverts all of them. It cannot be called only anyone of them — comedy, tragedy, comedy of humors, comedy of menace, kitchen—sink and absurd drama. The play disorients as Bernard F. Dukore is very relevant in this context: "A butcher cooks what one of his sons calls dog food. A young fighter is knocked down by his old father. A philosopher refuses to philosophize. A chauffeur is unable to drive. A pimp takes orders from his whore. The whore does not go all the way with a man. Words disorient, as when Lenny says of

Teddy, 'And my goodness we are proud of him here, I can tell you. Doctor of Philosophy and all that . . . leaves quite an impression.'" (III, 47) The first phrase appropriate to an old woman not a young man, the triteness of the phrase that ends the first sentence, 'and all that' belittling the advanced degree—these disorient, thereby conveying the impression that what is said is not what is meant. (77)

French philosopher, Jacque Derrida has definitely some influence on his contemporary playwright Pinter. The main concern of Derrida is to expose how language is fundamentally slippery, based on self–contradictory, unfinalizable conditions of difference and deference. Like Derrida's arguments, so far we have focused on the need to pay closer attention to the way in which meanings are produced temporarily rather than with any finality, through contradictions and ambivalence, and have consistently rebelled against any 'authoritative' or 'authoritarian' meaning. This final meaning which Derrida terms 'transcendental signified' is absent here but to establish this dictum there is a compulsion to fetch a little information from the author's biography and from some other areas of knowledge. Though deconstruction is theory that assumes language refers only to itself rather than to an external reality outside the text. There is nothing outside the text. In this, to some extent, deconstructive analysis of the play, we also have multiple, conflicting interpretations which are based on the language of the text itself, language that has philosophical, political and social implications. Pinter himself does not want his play to impose any significance beyond itself—yet the only proof which might have given it coherence and significance within itself is Ruth's speech: "Look at me. I . . . move my leg. That's all it is. But I wear . . . underwear . . . which moves with me . . . it captures your attention. Perhaps you misinterpret. The action is simple. It's a leg . . . moving. My lips move. Why don't you restrict . . . your observations to that? Perhaps the fact that they move is more significant . . . than the words which come through them. You must bear that . . . possibility . . . in mind." (60-61)

Through this playing on the word leg and the thing leg, on the word lips and the thing lips through which the words come to life, a distinction between the signifier and the signified is clearly made to establish the process of 'difference' (the way in which meaning differs from the words that try to express it and it is perpetually deferred). So here is a direct attack upon western metaphysics. Thus, the play is clearly rejecting totalizing narratives in favor of partial fragmented and incomplete ones and it falls under the umbrella of postmodern philosophy. In this way metaphysical foundation of all philosophical and moral certainties has been systematically undermined, when the supposedly stable cogito as the source of cognition and sovereignty of the self has been dismissed as a myth (Heidegger and Lacan), when the concept of history as a grand narrative of linear concatenation of events with underlying hidden meaning is demolished and replaced by 'archeology' and 'genealogy' (Foucault), when the written text is declared to have no univocal meaning and when the textual polysemy is vigorously emphasized (Derrida) and when thinking is considered as essentially nomadic and circular without any linearity or precise semantic destination (Deleuze). These are some of the bench-markers of the philosophical infrastructure which underpin the post-modern attitude to human condition that cause such explosion of meanings and they compel the postmodern playwright Harold Pinter to acknowledge the absence of 'Truth' (final meaning) in a roundabout way: "Truth in drama is forever elusive. You never quite find it but the search for it is compulsive. The search is clearly what drives the endeavour. The search is your task. More often than not you stumble upon the truth in the dark, colliding with it or just glimpsing an image or a shape which seems to correspond to the truth, often without realizing that you have done so. But the real truth is that there never is any such thing as one truth to be found in dramatic art. There are many. These truths challenge each other, recoil from each other, reflect each other, ignore each other, tease each other, are blind to each other. Sometimes you feel you have the truth of a moment in your hand, then it slips through your fingers and is lost." ('Harold Pinter: Art, Truth and Politics')

In this uncertain, unstable, absurd ambiance of the play, there is no shared experience and no common ground of understanding, though sometimes it turns up in camouflage using naturalistic dialogue and banal activities. Pinter has made traditional naturalism a kind of quicksand for existential despair. Arnold P. Hinchliffe is entirely correct when he says: "Pinter is concerned with humanity, love, necessity and contingency—not in a lunar landscape but in the slum-dwelling next door. He does not, however, fall into the trap of explaining everything in terms of a poor environment. His stress on impoverished backgrounds in the early plays is itself relative, underlining the fact that all material assets have a fundamental paucity." (36)

Pinter's primary concern is in the field of sensual and emotional experiences instead of the ground of moral, intellectual and spiritual experiences. They are rejected as they represent an order, a hope, a structure. There is no cosmic enlargement of human suffering. Rather it embodies the individual 'anxiety.' Man cannot 'bear very much reality; he cannot afford to be in an open space. He must seek a hide-out and force himself indoors, limiting his suffering within the walls of a cozy room, crowding his loneliness by memory or fancy. Without poking much into the incurable region of his private agony he would struggle to achieve extroversion. His speech may contain nonsense or even sheer lies, but he cannot afford to be depressed in his consciousness, he must speak and keep up the pretence of having established relationships. The fear is bone-deep, but the lips should not quiver. This disintegrated existence or the lifestyle is nothing but post-modernity. The result is that of a perpetual ambiguity — often presenting life as a muddle, full of local references rather than a mystery suggestive of cosmic and mythopoeic richness. And the overall impact is that of a special kind of pastiche—tragic in experience, comic in appearance, symbolic in essence and naturalistic on the surface.

The Birthday Party
A Futile Search for Meaning

The evolution of the English theatre in the 20th century encompasses a number of movements: 'social realistic,' 'poetic,' 'angry' and 'absurd.' Some rudimentary elements from each of these traditions have been assimilated by Harold Pinter to initiate a unique style of his own. But certain new forms of these provide a passionate denial of the general vocabulary and stock theatricality of traditional theatre. The new genre of poetic drama which attempted to regenerate the emotional power and creative intensity of Elizabethan plays petered out after a few dexterous, exciting and innovative efforts in the hands of Fry, T.S. Eliot, W.H. Auden and Isherwood. But they faced the major difficulty in reviving the hilarious conglomeration of realism, stylization and poetic emotions available in Shakespearean drama. To the realist theatre, it is impossible to acquire within itself the new feelings of disorientation and disintegration and it is rendered to confine itself to the 'low-life' comedy or 'kitchen-sink drama.' A few masterpieces such as John Osborne's *Look Back in Anger* was brought out by the theatre of 'angry young man' tradition, but this genre only tended to give birth to the period plays. Social drama, as in Arnold Wesker, acquired a few remarkable successes, but the social realist tradition was now hard - pressed in front of the challenge posited by continental experiments in drama. The 'free-theatres' accommodating different absurd plays of Eugene Ionesco, Jean Genet, Samuel Beckett and the 'epic—theatre' of Brecht patronized the directions of a new sensibility. A new verbal medium in response to this whole situation has been tended by the illusive dramatic language of Harold Pinter.

Pinter had more courage and dexterity than any other contemporary British dramatist to deal with the daring modern themes by adopting the European tradition to the requirements of a relatively more conservative British theatre and its audience. Different sorts of language component were infused in Pinter's naturalization of modernistic dramatic art: colloquial dialect which did not hamper the dramatic elegance and precision, poetic imagery which did not make tawdry display, absurd babblings, contradictions and repetitions which did not become over-stylized, and eloquence which did not turn up contrived and rhetorical so as to appear with lucidity. Pinter neither disowned his own tradition nor did he disavow the other contemporaries. He neither became a 'child of Godot' nor a 'Brechtian boy-scout.'

Unlike the previous chapter, where I have made an analysis adopting different situations, my chief concern here is to analyze his play *The Birthday Party* by taking it not fragmentarily but as a whole from some different post-structural point of view to show the contradictory meanings inherent in the play and the plurality of identity in a particular situation in disguise of the lack of identity.

The Birthday Party was the most emphatic of the early plays of Harold Pinter in regards of both theatrical and literary value. It did not become popular during its first production as an immediate sequel to the Bristol Production of *The Room* at the Arts Theatre in Cambridge in 1958 and subsequently at the Lyric Opera House in Hammersmith. It became successful to draw critical attention only after the review of it by *The Guardian* as a play "with all the dignity of a modern classic" (qtd. Hinchcliffe 123) in 1964 when produced in the Aldwych Theatre Summer Repertoire. But it was only Harold Hobson who recognized the bright future of the playwright while writing for *The Sunday Times* as early as 25 May 1958 and prognosticate the playwright's uniqueness: "Mr. Pinter, on the evidence of this work possesses the most original disturbing and arresting talent in theatrical London" (qtd. In Lloyd Evans

63). Among other reasons, the play's being 'disturbing' yet 'arresting' speaks about the shifting moods that this play aroused in the mind of the spectators. In the amusement at the travesty of a birthday party there is the shadow of menace of the crisis of identity. Piquancy of daily colloquialism makes patterns of contrast and confrontation and so the mundane takes a violent turn—these shifting moods of the play characterize the realm of tragicomedy.

Here I do not want to add yet the same label to the already existing list many times ascribed to this play, such as 'absurdist,' 'tragicomedy,' 'dark comedy' or a 'comedy of menace.' These tags encircle him within the periphery of the avant-grade category and obfuscate the original theatrical potential of his plays. This chapter aims at viewing *The Birthday Party* from three apparently contradicted point of view though there is a submerged thread which connects them: how the dramatic genre of the tragicomedy within the premises of *The Birthday Party* has readily accommodated the needs of the changing world-order of postmodernism, confrontation of an existential man with the 'Big Brother' of the colonial society and the forceful conformation of this individual, and finally the psychoanalytical overview of the dramatic characters. The connecting thread is here the excellent manipulation of the identity politics.

Tragicomedy

Encompassing a vast sphere from Plautus's *Amphitryon* or Giambattista Guarini's *IL Pastor Fido* to Samuel Beckett's *Waiting for Godot*, tragicomedy as a dramatic genre asserted itself best amidst conflict. The genre flourished during 1605-1650 in the Jacobean–Caroline age especially in the works of Beaumont and Fletcher, Ben Jonson and William Shakespeare. It emphasized the strain of gross materialism and skepticism underneath the Renaissance tide of optimism and individualism. This same crisis has been reinstated in the modern age too as T.S. Eliot says it the "immense panorama of anarchy and futility" (166). In the philosophical realms of Existentialism and the Absurd this concept is clearly reiterated as Albert Camus illustrates in *The Myth of Sisyphus*: "in a universe that is suddenly deprived of illusions and of light man feels a stranger. His is an irremediable exile. . . This divorce between man and his life, the actor and his setting, truly constitutes the feeling of Absurdity" (28).

Another major philosopher of Existentialism, Kierkegaard, accepts modern existence as essentially tragicomic, "Existence itself, the act of existence, is a striving and is both pathetic and comic in the same degree" (qtd. In Wilson 290). For the same reason *Waiting for Godot* has been called by Beckett himself 'a tragicomedy in two acts' (3). However, Harold Pinter never publicly calls his plays tragicomedies. Nevertheless, he does not hesitate to acknowledge the mixed nature of their emotional impact: "Everything is funny; the greatest earnestness is funny; even tragedy is funny. And I think what I try to do in my plays is to get this recognizable of the absurdity of what we do and how we behave and how we speak." (qtd. *The Theatre of the Absurd* 242)

To illuminate the tragicomic mood of his plays Pinter here willingly uses such ambiguous words like funny. He again states, "The point about tragedy is that it is no longer funny. It is funny, and then it becomes no longer funny" (242). Life is funny because it is arbitrary, based on illusions and self-deceptions, like Stanley's dream that he is going on a world tour as a pianist, because it is built out of pretence and the grotesque over-estimation each individual makes of himself. This sort of bad faith is more or less the constant companion of all of us. Whatever his characters constantly use this open-ended word 'funny.' Davies in the *Caretaker* and Stanley in *The Birthday Party* use it in the respective plays to develop the important tragicomic perceptions. In this context, we must mention that Bernard F. Dukore in *Where Laughter Stops: Pinter's Tragicomedy* attempts to locate a specific moment within each of Pinter's plays where the forces of tragedy overpower the forces of comedy (5). There is no doubt that his analysis underscores the tragicomic movement of Pinter's plays. However, he also misses a crucial point: the complications and subtlety of Pinter's versions of tragicomedy hide in the fact that situations can be simultaneously happy and unhappy, hilarious and baffling, familiar and grotesque. Sometimes the sources of this comic and tragic may be the same.

> GOLDBERG (to LULU). Enjoying the game?
> MEG. It's your turn, Stan.
> MCCANN takes off the scarf.
> MCCANN (to STANLEY). I'll take your glasses.
> MCCANN takes STANLEY'S glasses.
> MEG. Give me the scarf.
> GOLDBERG (holding LULU). Tie his scarf, Mrs. Boles.
> MEG. That's what I'm doing. (To STANLEY.) Can you see my nose?
> GOLDBERG. He can't. Ready? Right! Everyone moves. Stop! And still!
> *Stanley stands blindfold. Mccann backs slowly across the stage to the left. He breaks Stanley's glasses, snapping the frames. Meg is downstage, left, Lulu and Goldberg upstage centre, close together. Stanley begins to move, very slowly, across the stage to the left. Mccann picks up the drum and places it sideways in Stanley's path. Stanley walks into the drum and falls over with his foot caught in it.* (II, 63)

In these moments of 'enjoying the game' of blind man's bluff, there is a terrible thing done by Mccann—the glasses of Stanley have been broken and thus his vision has been usurped by the intruders. Taking into consideration this distinctive feature of Pinter's early plays, we would see how Pinter handles several generic implications and mixes them in *The Birthday Party*. The tragic, comic or the farcical are mingled within the mocking investigative analogies or the mystery thriller or detective story or suspense film. The profanity and laughter of the music hall and vaudeville tradition are mixed with pantomimes, black comedy or grotesque *danse macabre* of the Jacobean tragicomedy. Yet all of these are very subtly assimilated to the permeating absurdist world-view that accounts for the metaphysical anguish and sense of rootlessness in postmodern man; and it finally leads the playwright to indulge in an open-ended closure in his play.

The play arouses a lot of questions in the minds of the theatre-goers. At the end of the play the audience is spell-bound just like Stanley. At the end of the play Stanley has been reduced to an automaton just like Lucky in *Waiting for Godot* who loses even his speaking ability. The play ends with Meg and Petey's paradoxical detachment about the whole affair. Pinter willingly creates the loopholes in the play regarding the past of Stanley and the intruders. Even at the end we are overwhelmed by the burden of the questions aroused in our mind—what is Stanley's guilt and where has he been taken? Is it a regenerative second birth for Stanley? Is the birthday party nothing but a death-knell for the protagonist? Is it a genuine birthday or an absurd misrepresentation? These questions have not a rigid, definite, monolithic answer but they have multiple probable answers. As a postmodern writer Pinter himself has incredulity towards the concept of truth. But he cannot forego it. He himself says, "There are no hard distinctions between what is real and what is unreal, nor between what is true and what is false. A thing is not necessarily either true or false; it can be both true and false." (qtd. the Nobel Prize winning speech)

The trite conversation of the Boles about cornflakes and family routine in the play's beginning appears comic. Its verbal humor depends upon Pinter's dialogic art of repetition. Meg's repetitive question to Petey and again in another context to Stanley 'is that you?' clearly suggests Meg's identification of his familiars with their voice. Meg's repetitive queries to Petey 'I've got your cornflakes ready. Here is your cornflakes' (1, 9) and her all-purpose 'nice' (that recurs almost ten times within the first three pages of dialogue) possess the naturalistic gloss of creating the 'slice-of-life' realism. It is natural for the audience—aware of the contemporary 'kitchen-sink' style of Alum Owen or Arnold Wesker—to expect another conventional play of middle-class or low-class life. Stanley's shabby presence on stage and his queer cajoling with his land lady not only project a mother-son relationship but also ironically imply an illicit love affair. So here begins first the politics of identity in the play. When Meg says, "I am going to wake that boy" (I, 13) and when she treats Stanley as a mother treats her child, when she says, "Stan! I'm coming up to fetch you if you don't come down!" (I, 13) and also when Stanley shouts after Meg's laughing wildly, the audience naturally expects a boy. But what is again shocking is that Stanley appears to be "not a boy, but a bespectacled groggy man in his pyjama jacket" (Dukore, *Modern Dramatists* 32). Pinter here begins his politics of identity in the mother-son relationship. Even the breakfast of both Petey and Stanley is 'cornflakes,' usually a food for children (9). The responses of Petey and Stanley in relation to the breakfast are comic:

> MEG. I've got your cornflakes ready. Here's your cornflakes. Are they nice?
> PETEY. Very nice. (I, 9)

But Stanley's response to Meg suggests that Stanley does not want to do what Meg wants him to do. Although lack of communication is not the major theme of the play, the following conversation suggests that Stanley behaves towards Meg rather casually without that warmth Meg feels for him:

> MEG. What are the cornflakes like, Stan?
> STANLEY. Horrible.
> MEG. Those flakes? Those lovely flakes? You're a liar, a little liar. They're refreshing. It says so. For people when they get up late.
> STANLEY. The milk's off. (I, 15)

Again, when Meg demands that her boarding house is very well known, Stanley denies her. Although the house is, according to Meg, "on the list", Stanley rejects that claim by saying that he is only her visitor: "Me! I'm your visitor" (I, 17). Meg asks Stanley if "the fried bread" is nice. Stanley replies: "Succulent" (I, 17). This word is a typical example of Pinteresque wordplay. Words in his plays change their meanings in different situations, as they do in poetry, operating at different levels of eloquence in different characters. Pinter has a kind of mixed-feeling about language. He takes delight in the poetic potential of words. But he also finds much that is repugnant about words which uncontrollably relate to a stale stock of overtones having been used in certain contexts for generations. He seems to experience both a sense of joy and feeling of nausea in his contact with words. The meaning of a Pinter-play is often located in this tension between delight and revulsion with reference to the words which body forth the dramatic emotion. Whatever, Stanley's reply 'succulent' means juicy and tasting good. Although it is an innocuous word, it is given sensual overtones by Meg's reaction: "You shouldn't say that word to a married woman" (I, 17). She seems to be sensual, though her feelings for Stanley throughout the three acts appear to be that of an affectionate mother. When Stanley, much annoyed, calls her "You succulent old washing bag" (I, 18), and asks her to leave him, Meg reacts to the remark rather sensually:

> MEG. Stan?
> STANLEY. What?
> MEG (shyly). Am I really succulent? (I, 19)

Meg, of course, confuses the term "succulent". Her affection for Stanley is disturbing. Stanley tries to keep her always at a distance. It, therefore, proves improbability of any sexual relationship between them, in spite of the innuendo, "I've had some lovely afternoons in that room" (I, 19). Although Meg's attentions to Stanley are insufferable and irritating, her affection for him is more genuine, and it resembles a mother's affection for her child. Meg seems to be a mother-surrogate. She reveals her wish to her husband Petey: "I'd much rather have a little boy" (I, 11). Even she does not want Stanley to go to "the palace, in the town" to enjoy a new show (I, 13). She is quite reluctant to allow Stanley to go out of her sight. Thus, she says to Petey "Stanley could have been in it, if it was on the pier" (I, 13). This, in fact, refers to the prenatal leash. Rightly does Bill Naismith admit that "the mother-son relationship is much more compelling" (55).

But what brings about the suspension of belief are the arbitrary declaration of birthday, Stanley's unverifiable account of his past. Pinter himself says, what basically baffles us is "the immense difficulties if not impossible of verifying the past" ('Programme Note for *The Caretaker*' 41). The following speeches are relevant in this context:

> STANLEY. I've . . . er . . . I've been offered a job, as a matter of fact.
> MEG. What?
> STANLEY. Yes. I'm considering a job at the moment.
> MEG. You're not.
> STANLEY. A good one, too. A night club. In Berlin.
> MEG. Berlin?
> STANLEY. Berlin. A night club. Playing the piano. A fabulous salary. And all found.
> MEG. How long for?
> STANLEY. We don't stay in Berlin. Then we go to Athens.
> MEG. How long for?
> STANLEY. Yes. Then we pay a flying visit to . . . er . . . whatsisname. . . MEG. Where?
> STANLEY. Constantinople. Zagreb. Vladivostok. It's a round the world tour.
> MEG. Have you played the piano in those places before?
> STANLEY. Played the piano? I've played the piano all over the world. All over the country. (*pause*) I once gave a concert. (I 22)

In a ludicrous way Stanley briefly describes his career as a pianist. He gradually reduces his playing of piano throughout the world to giving them all over the country and to finally giving a concert just 'once.' The unreliability reflects the inability of language to express and communicate human experience. Hence, we notice how Pinter utilizes the rhythms of everyday speech to drive at something completely different.

With the progress of the play Pinter leaves elements of strangeness one by one. The oblique sense of menace and violence was anticipated vaguely in Stanley's teasing Meg with a threat of two men:

> STANLEY (advancing): They are coming today.
> MEG: Who?
> STANLEY: They are coming in a van.
> MEG: Who?
> STNLEY: And do you know what they've got in that van?
> MEG: What?
> STANLEY: They've got a wheelbarrow in that van.
> MEG (breathlessly): They haven't.
> STANLEY: Oh yes, they have.
> MEG: You're a liar.
> STANLEY (advancing upon her): A big wheelbarrow. And when the van stops they wheel it out, and they wheel it up the garden path, and then they knock at the front door.
> MEG: They don't.
> STANLEY: They're looking for someone.
> MEG: They're not.
> STANLEY: They're looking for someone. A certain person.
> MEG (hoarsely): No, they're not!
> STANLEY: Shall I tell you who they're looking for?
> MEG: No!
> STANLEY: You don't want me to tell you?
> MEG: You're a liar! (I, 24)

The van with the wheelbarrow in it, with which Stanley frightens Meg, may be a hearse with a coffin. Stanley does not mention specifically who is the person to be taken away. Maybe it is Meg and so Meg's reaction comes of her fear of her own death. Here Stanley is just playing the role of a psycho-terrorist just like Goldberg who may be worthy of his mentor in this game. Here he is the victor and Meg is the victim. But Stanley may also imply the prospect of his own disappearance. From the next part of the play, we would be made quite sure that Stanley's imagined fear is nothing but his own fear of being revenged by the complicity of his past. In Pinter's another drama *The Room*, Rose's fear of losing her secure, warm, comfortable room is nothing but the fear of losing her life and hence the coming of the Negro at her home is clearly the signal of her impending doom. Both of the protagonists (Stanley and Rose) finally have become blind. Stanley's accurate dress, his losing of speech and vision actually draw a picture of him lying in the grave as a corpse. Goldberg's black car at the end would therefore surely represent a hearse and Stanley's black suit the shroud. The two intruders in their boarding house thus may also symbolize the two harbingers of the God of death and they have been sent to transport a human being into the nether world. So, like Martin Esslin in his *Pinter The Playwright*, we can also view the superior Goldberg as a strange caricature of Jehovah, the Lord over life and death for his pronounced Jewish family feelings and sentimentality whereas the cruel tormentor Mccann may represent the projection of Stanley's menace towards the physical suffering in the hour of extinction.

Our suspicion of their being messengers of death are established later in the play with Goldberg's symbolic reassertion - 'you're dead. You can't live.' (II, 52) Indeed his dark car is found outside their house and it finally carries Stanley off. In the opening scene of the play this story which is told quite light-heartedly or even comically (Stanley may be playing his pranks of bewildering Meg or casually frightening her with this story) assumes serious overtones after a point. It establishes our point—the very sources of the comic and non-comic are the same and finally the initial comedy is thoroughly subverted.

Pinter tactfully uses his elements of pantomime to sum up Stanley's protest against Meg's off-handedly thrusting upon him a 'birthday' and her gift of a child's play drum. In this regard we should closely follow the playwright's following stage directions: "He hangs a drum around his neck, taps it gently with sticks, then marches round the table beating it regularly. Meg, pleased, watches him. Still beating it regularly, he begins to go round the table a second time. Halfway round the beat becomes erratic, uncontrolled. MEG expresses dismay. He arrives at her chair, banging the drum, and his face and the drumbeat now savage and possessed." (I, 36)

From it we easily perceive that this situation is an example of 'objective correlative'[1] of Stanley's over saturated nerves. The gradually increasing sound of the drumbeat makes the replica of the restlessness and bewilderment of Stanley's mind. It is the only form of protest however diminutive, which is possible from Stanley. Pantomimes which are generally performed by stand-up comedians are underscored with comic implications. In the rising rhythm of Stanley's toy-drum the grotesque and violent are combined. It evokes what Nicholas Brooke calls 'the horrid laughter' (2). Moreover, the beating of the drum is a device of the hunter of violent animals, to frighten and send it to the corner before pouncing upon it. Just like the previous chapter, the animal metaphor is here equally employed in case of Stanley as he is unable to utter a single meaningful word of language and merely utters animal mumbling at the end of the play. The irony applied here is that the signal of predation is given not by the hunters but by the victim himself. Stanley, in spite of his categorical assertion, 'this not my birthday, Meg,' unwillingly accepts her gift of the child drum and starts to beat it and knells his own doom. Here it is notable that Pinter uses some expressionistic methods to convey the psychosis of the victim of the play.

The stichomythic interrogation scene is the central scene of the play rather than the ceremony of the birthday party itself, because it shows the relationships of the characters to each other and the nature of the power struggle involved in the drama. The chief concern of the play, that is, the oppressive forces of conformism (though not clearly stated) are most evidently articulated here. This scene indirectly states that probably Stanley was a member of some organization and he has 'betrayed' or offended them. So, Goldberg and Mccann may be the agents of this organization and they have been sent to make Stanley account for his guilt and to re-assimilate him into that system from which he escaped. They begin their attack by leveling him general accusations of contempt for accepted social order (killing his wife, rejection of his mother, lechery, a dishonest trade) and arouse these to a frenzy with the demands of logic ('Is the number 846 possible or necessary' [II, 50]) and nonsense ('what about the blessed Oliver Plunkett? [II, 51]). The playwright vaguely entangled Staley with Mccann's Irishness and Goldberg's Jewishness and then developed it into accusations of treason ('what about Ireland [. . .] What about Drogheda?' [II, 51-52]) And atheism ('you stink of sin [. . .] Do you recognize an external force [. . .] When did you last pray?' [II, 50]). A rejection of the essentially reactionary demands of church and patriotism creates the cornerstone of Stanley's transgression. The Jewish and Irish are the representatives of two historically abused people and two ideologically inflexible religions. They end their verbal operation by casting Stanley in the worst of moulds and follow through by exposing his triteness.

> MCCANN. You betrayed our land.
> GOLDBERG. You betray our breed.
> MCCANN. Who are you, webber?
> GOLDBERG. What makes you think you exist?
> MCCANN. You're dead.
> GOLDBERG. You're dead. You can't live, you can't think, you can't love. You're dead, you're a plague gone bad. There's no juice in you. You're nothing but an odour! (II, 52)

Here the oppressive force is nothing but the illogically and violently used language. Here lie the basic precepts of existential philosophy. Not only those, but also the questions—"Do you recognize an external force responsible for you?" (II, 50) and "Chicken?

Egg? Which came first?" (II, 52)—pertain two existentialist queries. Through Goldberg and Mccann's uncanny interrogation, Pinter incorporates the existential proposition that man does not come to earth tagged with an identity. It is clearly related to the basic concept of Existentialism. Man is born in *Le neant* (darkness) and *Le visqueux* (mud) of ignorance. But as he grows up, the ignorance is lost and simultaneously he gains the anxiety of the search for the self—a very intricate self. It is the anxiety for the true identity. As an existentialist, Pinter exploits the issues of identity, communication and sanity but as a postmodern writer, he deliberately undercuts their seriousness by treating them farcical. Generally, these questions not only underplay and mock the sacredness of the previous issues but, being the awkward gathering of verbal jumble, they immediately provoke laughter. Pinter's interrogation pattern with the non-sequitur questions suggests an interesting parallel with a passage from Beckett's *Waiting for Godot:*

> VLADIMIR. I interrupted you.
> ESTRAGON. I interrupted you.
> VLADIMIR. On the contrary. They glare at each other angrily. . .
> ESTRAGON. What do you do now?
> VLADIMIR. While waiting.
> ESTRAGON. While waiting.
> VLADIMIR. We could do our exercises.
> ESTRAGON. Our movements.
> VLADIMIR. Our elevations.
> ESTRAGON. Our relaxation.
> VLADIMIR. Our elongations.
> ESTRAGON. Our relaxations. (75-76).

It exhibits that both Pinter and Beckett were experimenting to adapt and refurbish the tragicomic form in the modern context.

It would be very exciting to compare the ordeal of Stanley with the murder of Thomas Beckett in T.S. Eliot's *Murder in the Cathedral. The Birthday Party* has also the elements of ritual in its structure. The sacrificial rites in the scapegoat figure of the myth of regeneration may have been re-enacted in the machinations and manipulations employed by Goldberg and Mccann to collapse Stanley's self-integrity and identity. The brutal interrogation of Stanley and his consequent disintegration in the party actually parodies the temptation of Thomas Becket followed by the knight's ritualistic sacrifice of the martyr. No rejuvenation of society can happen with Stanley's suffering. Instead, he is such a diminutive protagonist that he cannot even invoke awe and wonder in the mind of the audience, because he is essentially inarticulate. In his letter to Peter Wood in 1958 Harold Pinter wrote about his protagonist: "Stanley fights for his life, he does not want to be drowned. Who does? But he is not articulate. . . Stanley cannot perceive his only valid justification which is, he is what he is—therefore he can never be articulate about it. He knows only to attempt to justify himself by dream, by pretence and by bluff, through fright. . . Stanley is the king of his castle and loses his kingdom because he assessed it and himself inaccurately." (Casebook 80-81)

It is the unique feature of post-structural tragedy to draw reminiscences of the tragedy and simultaneously to underplay parody and refashion its effect. It is very much adjusted with the modern world order which compels the individual to indulge in deception. It forces man to have less faith in his own self, own mind but to have more fear for the outside dehumanizing forces.

Unlike the conclusion of the traditional tragicomedy, that is, upholding the flag of humanity, this tragicomedy of modern age with post-modern vision ends with the degeneration of the protagonist and also with his futile attempt at speech through animal groaning: "uh huh. . . uh—gug" (III, 84). The open-ended closure of it evokes several questions—where has Stanley been taken away? Finally what happens to him? Thus, the experience of watching the play for the spectators is tragicomic or what Pinter himself states, as 'funny.'

In this regard we have an interesting resemblance between *The Birthday Party* and Eugene O'Neill's *The Iceman Cometh*. O'Neill's impact on Pinter would be evident if we compare Pinter's previous comment with the following remark of O'Neill: "There is a feeling around or I'm mistaken of fate—Kismet the negative fate, not in the Greek sense. . . It's struck me as time goes on, how something funny, even farcical can suddenly without any apparent reason break up into something gloomy and tragic. . .I think I'm aware of comedy that doesn't stay funny very long. I've made some use of it in *The Iceman.* The first act is hilarious, I think, but then some people may not even laugh. At any rate, the comedy tracks up and tragedy comes." (Gelb 488).

Such tragicomic perspectives of both the playwrights of different traditions are manifested a little subtly in the two dramas' counterpoint where cornflakes, drums, birthdays and games are played out respectively against the growing degenerations of humanity. The impact of the tragic counterpart is clearly exposed in cowardly Petey's vain protest: "Stan, don't let them tell you what to do" (III, 86) and also in the equally craven drunken Larry's sharing with the audience in *The Iceman Cometh*. Though the baffling end of the play has plurality of meaning, the apparent image of triumph is also visible in Meg's last lines, in her reminiscing of the "lovely party" (III, 87) of the last night at which she was the "belle of the ball" (III, 87). We can say from it that this profoundly meaningful, poignantly ironic ending actually pokes the happy ending of a traditional tragicomedy.

In *The Birthday Party*, Pinter redefines and remodels the generic qualities as well as the limitations of modern tragicomedy. Pinter belongs to the absurdist genre and no doubt his writing is imbued with absurdist features but he never obstinately follows the illogical, grotesque devices of absurdist drama. Instead, he intermingles and re-moulds conventional tragicomic elements with other popular dramatic and cultural forms in this play (like the forms of the farce, parody, music-hall or vaudeville, the pantomime or the detective story and the carnivalesque) and thus his literary journey gets a junction in this play as from here he takes a turn towards postmodernism leaving behind him the modernism.

Role-Playing and Game-Playing

In *The Birthday Party*, Pinter refashions certain theatrical strategies and cultural archetypes that characteristically belonged to the Elizabethan and Jacobean drama. We would particularly illuminate Pinter's use of the role playing and game playing mechanism in this play. In this connection I have to re-mention that there is a common thematic base that justifies both these strategies—the problem of identity and its security. Human identity is constantly questioned in both the clichés.

Role playing in *The Birthday Party* is not merely extraneous to its dramatic form; rather its presence is also within the play's framework. In our everyday life, there is always a gap between the appearance and reality; always a spasm between the created image of a man and his inner self. Man always tries to create for himself a good identity, but the role he plays in his actual life more or less differs from his created identity. In this play we find it in Goldberg's prudishness: "When I was a youngster, on a Friday, I used to go for a walk down the canal with a girl who lived down my road. A beautiful girl. What a voice that bird had! A nightingale, my word of honour. Good? Pure? She wasn't a Sunday school teacher for nothing. Anyway, I'd leave her with a little kiss on the cheek—I never took liberties—we weren't like the young men these days. We knew the meaning of respect. So I'd give her a peck and I'd bowl back home. Humming away I'd be, past the children's playground. I'd tip my hat to the toddlers, I'd give a helping hand to a couple of stray dogs, everything came natural." (II, 43)

By this description of his past, Goldberg wants to create an image of humbleness. But in his action, we find a completely different man who victimizes Stanley brutally and sexually assaults Lulu uncivilly. Stanley also indulges in role playing with his unreliable account of his past. But he is not such a good player as his tormentor. Both of them use rhetoric in their language for role playing and thereby create different identities. But here is also a very subtle power politics. Only the powerful have the right to do so. If one is found doing it with the more powerful, it would be questioned and the wrong-doer would be punished. It is vaguely found in the context of Stanley in the interrogation scene where Stanley is questioned by a better player of this game, a worse sinner in this hell:

> GOLDBERG. Webber! Why did you change your name?
> STANLEY. I forgot the other one.
> GOLDBERG. What's your name now?
> STANLEY. Joe Soap.
> GOLDBERG. You stink of sin.
> MCCANN. I can smell it. (II, 50)

Goldberg too, ascribes himself various names like 'Nat,' 'Simey' and 'Benny' to demarcate separate identities associated with different phases of life and different types of persons. Mccann is also referred to as 'Seamus' and 'Dermot' and his identity is also uncertain in the play. But the player, sometimes, is also entangled subjectively in this game as this dual role of acting and reality begins to confuse him too. It is established, when we see Goldberg rebuffing violently when Mccann calls him 'Nat.' Goldberg can associate this name with his mother, his childhood memories, and his innocent phase of life. His inner self has been vexed by its association with his complicit, his complicated phase of life. Here Pinter attempts to explore the fragmented mental and psychological landscape of post-modern man within his formal limits of theatrical credibility.

The other trope–game playing may be viewed as an extension of role playing because game playing assumes a certain system in which the individuals want to play their intended role in disguise of a prescribed role. Taking into account its cultural ramification, Eric Berne in his *Games People Play* shows how games in general, attempt to conceal an "ulterior quantity"—their "lurking motivation" or "underlying snare" (44) beneath the façade of their ritualistic festivities. It is just like the theoretical concept of Mikhail Bakhtin's 'carnivalesque. Bakhtin, in his book *Rabelais and His World,* uses the term to refer to the celebrations during which not only commoners but also the more privileged classes are temporarily free to transgress all kinds of written, unwritten, social and Ecclesiastical laws. The discourse of carnival consists of the down-to-earth priorities and values of the unprivileged or plebeian 'second world' commoners or folk. That world is necessarily associated with the basic issues of survival, with the sustenance and reproduction of life. It is substantially concerned with the body, eating, sex and death; characteristically playful, it typically involves sensuous imagery. This play's characters are not the plebian. Their party motif in the play is not the desire of eating, but to generate the carnal desire of lechery, bear-baiting and violence. All of these are passing in the name of party fun. It is actually the wish fulfillment of temporary liberation from society's established order and prevailing truth. Both of these theatrical strategies explore the technique of play within a play. For example, the scene of 'game of chess' in *Women Beware Women* by Thomas Middleton is a play within a play and in this scene Bianca, in the background, is being seduced by the duke, while in the foreground Livia, the duke's accomplice, plays a game of chess with Bianca's mother-in-law in order to hold her attention. Every move in the game corresponds to a step in the forcible seduction of Bianca. So, the real intention is hidden.

All these features are accommodated in the game of blind man's bluff played in the birthday party of Stanley. It is a traditional party game and so is suitable for that occasion of birthday. But behind the civilized connotations of the party game, its darkness and blindness have been strategically used to bring about

Stanley's 'nervous breakdown' (III, 71). Each and every character has their different motives. To Meg, it vents her motherly impulses for Stanley and it executes her dream to be the 'belle of the ball.' Goldberg utilizes the darkness to seduce Lulu as a passing fancy only to satisfy his carnal 'appetite.' It gives Mccann the chance to lynch Stanley's self-integrity. Mccann, in the party game, becomes able to break Stanley's glasses along with his toy drum. The game is not only the crater for the hostile impulses of the tormentors but also for Stanley himself. His seeking to strangle Meg or assault Lulu sexually may be accepted as desperate protests of the marginalized victim who is goaded to the verge of dementia and depersonalization. Another representative of this type may be seen in much later Indian play *Silence! The Court is in Session* by Vijay Tendulkar. Through the same device of game playing Lila Benare is trapped and jeopardized by her male associates of her theatre-group the Sonarmoti Tenement (Bombay) Association in the play.

The Existential Crisis

The crime or misdeed of the past coming to agitate the present of an individual is a very age-old theme in literature. The most influential modern work in this subject is Franz Kafka's novel *The Trial* which begins, "Someone must have traduced Joseph K., for without having done anything wrong he was arrested one fine morning" (3). There is a fine similarity between the two protagonists—Stanley and Joseph K. both of whom attract two strangers to arrest them on the fine morning of their birthday. The arresting agents in both cases involve language games and they have their unspecified, invisible superiors, like the 'Big Brother' of George Orwell's *1984*, who seem to represent the establishment. Both Stanley and Joseph K. suffer from paranoia. During the twentieth century, the more the power of the state increases the more the individual becomes marginalized and distanced from the centers of power. Arthur Miller has cited many examples of how this power has operated against the individual in the modern world and finds the root of the discourse, that is, the government is a holy entity and individual the unholy one. The worst instances of it are Hitler, Stalin, Mccarthy.

But what is Stanley's guilt? There is no implication that Stanley has been a danger to the system of state or has threatened it anyway. It is not directly of political nature yet we have to be sure that he has offended that holy entity, the unspecified authorities whose agents are Goldberg and Mccann. Pinter himself has stated that Stanley has discarded the responsibility towards himself and others. He has opted out, and so definitely society takes revenge. It is his fault. In this drama, the individual is crushed below the weight of social expectations, rather than specific tyranny. In an interview with Mel Gussow, Pinter says that the play showed how the 'bastard,' that is, the religious forces ruin our lives. So maybe it is the oppressive religious forces working.

Goldberg and Mccann represent the Judeo-Christian tradition in Western civilization which demands conformity towards family, state and church. So, Goldberg turns up as a highly sociable fellow and so he suggests that they should give Stanley a party for his birthday. But who is Goldberg to give Stanley a birthday party? There are some obscure connections which operate like a poetic imagery joining Stanley and Goldberg. Goldberg speaks about his uncle Barney who "had a house just outside Basingstoke" (I, 27). Later Stanley pleads to Mccann by saying, "I've explained to you, damn you, that all those years I lived in Basingstoke I have never stepped outside the door" (III, 42). Similar to this, here is also a connection between them:

> STANLEY. I've got a feeling we've met before.
> MCCANN. No, we haven't.
> STANLEY. Ever been anywhere near Maidenhead?
> MCCANN. No.
> STANLEY. There's a Fuller's teashop. I used to have my tea there.
> MCCANN. I don't know.

> STANLEY. And a Boots Library. I seem to connect you with the High Street. (II, 39)

After sometime Goldberg refers to it, "A little Austin, tea in Fuller's, a Library book from Boots, and I am satisfied." (II, 56) I think this is not a coincidence, rather it is a surreal connection. It symbolizes that Goldberg and Mccann may be considered imaginatively as figments of Stanley's subconscious guilt. So, they may be the symbolic fictional stage characters. So here I completely agree with Katherine Worth's suggestion: "Pinter brilliantly conveys the suggestion that the inquisitors are unreal beings, a projection of Stanley's obscure dread, without quite destroying the possibility of their being taken as real; this is what makes them so alarming." (Casebook 37)

In his poem 'A View of the Party' (published in the year of the first performance of the play), Pinter himself places Goldberg into the power center:

> The thought that Goldberg was
> A man he might have known
> Never crossed Meg's words
> That morning in the room.
>
> The thought that Goldberg was
> A man another knew
> Never crossed her eyes
> When, glad, she welcomed him.
>
> The thought that Goldberg was
> A man to dread and know
> Jarred Stanley in the blood
> When, still, he heard his name. (Casebook 83)

By doing so, Pinter makes Goldberg more than merely the representative of the evil power pursuing Stanley; but he makes him the incarnation of the power itself. But in the second part of the poem, the sound of Katherine Worth is resonant—the intruders might be forces in the mind—thoughts:

> The thought that Goldberg was
> Sat in the centre of the room,
> A man of weight and time,
> To supervise the game.
>
> The thought that was McCann
> Walked in upon this feast,
> A man of skin and bone,
> With a green stain on his chest. (Casebook 83-84)

The menace in the play completely resides in Goldberg and Mccann. Now the question is what does their organization represent? Most frequently they are viewed as the forces of society and convention who, at the price of the sacrifice of Stanley's inner being, will bestow him "a new, prosperous and socially approved life" (Dukore, *Where Laughter Stops* 16).

> GOLDBERG. We'll make a man of you.
> MCCANN. And a woman.
> GOLDBERG. You'll be re-oriented.
> MCCANN. You'll be rich.
> GOLDBERG. You'll be adjusted.
> MCCANN. You'll be pride and joy.
> GOLDBERG. You'll be a mensch
> MCCANN. You'll be a success.
> GOLDBERG. You'll be integrated.
> MCCANN. You'll give orders. (III, 83-84)

Martin Esslin in his *Pinter the Playwright* gives another suggestion: "it is fairly clear—particularly from the final image of Stanley in the uniform of respectable, bourgeois gentility—that Stanley is the artist whom society claims back from a comfortable, bohemian, 'opt-out' existence. This, it seems, is possible because he is an artist who has doubts about his creative ability; he has not worked for a long time; he has come down, from a piano to a little boy's drum; and even that he breaks in his clumsiness in the game of blind man's bluff." (72-73)

So, in this regard, the breaking of the toy drum is not the symbolic destruction of his artistic identity, rather it may be the initiation of the recovery of his artistic identity which 'society claims back.' This other side of menace would be discussed in detail in the next sub-chapter.

Thus, we can illustrate the peril of Stanley as the hellish demands of the adult world upon a reluctant adolescent forced to leave the childhood security. There are enormous interpretations of it. The intruders may also be the representatives of inevitable death which caps the futile existence. So, Goldberg admits, "If we hadn't come to day we'd have come tomorrow" (I, 32). It is also suggestive of the birth itself: "An expulsion from the Edenic womb" (Batty 96). Whatever, they do not let Stanley live according to his own free will. Bill Naismith rightly comments: "He is not permitted to be himself, whatever and whoever he is. Goldberg and Mccann effectively destroy his identity and transform him into the visual representation of respectable society—'dressed in a dark well- cut suit and white collar.' In appearance he is completely altered, but in fact he has become dehumanized because he has lost the definitive mark of identity—the power of human speech." (47)

The play *The Birthday Party* may point to not only all the above interpretations but also other similar perspectives. But behind its back, what the play actually does is nothing but to evoke the 'shape' of such experiences. The word 'shape' avoids the kinds of specificity that these interpretations thrust individually and which Pinter's structures effectively avoid too. To conclude, nothing is better than referring Mark Batty: "It is the shape of active invading forces that diminish the resistance of latent desires and potentials, reducing these to obedience and conformity. It is the shape of unchecked authority that sneers at weakness and equates individuality with sedition. Our ability to recognize such structures in operation in our interpersonal relationships, in our society's infrastructure and in our country's political discourses provides us with a daily forum for ethical and moral consideration." (97)

Is the External Force Liberating?

This external oppressive force of conformism would be no longer evil if we look at it from Arthur Ganz's point of view. Ganz wrote in his *Realms of the Self: Variations on a Theme in Modern Drama*—the "disintegrating lassitude that Stanley has lapsed into at the beginning of *The Birthday Party*, for example, is hardly preferable to the bumptious certainties and brutish sentimentalities of Goldberg and Mccann" (193). Surely Ganz does not drift down in the stream of the general criticism of Pinter. Ganz has become a notable exception by claiming that Goldberg and Mccann are not the villains but rather are vital forces who turn up "not, like the organized assassins they appear to be, to remove Stanley from the living but to do no less than to raise him from the dead" (196). I think it would be very helpful to us if we take the menace aroused by Goldberg and Mccann as a threatening force of a conscious guardian, which shows another way to Stanley in his search for self-identity. This point of view explores that Pinter presents in the play two alternative but equally impossible contexts for the discovery of himself—one personal and the other social. Hence the real fear is not that Stanley is collapsed at the end of the play, but that he would be also destroyed if he remains there any longer.

If Stanley has been diminished at the end of the play as a washed and walking cadaver, he is similarly reduced as an object at the beginning of the play, as he fully fills Meg's requirement to have a man-child to satisfy her mothering and also sexual drives. That is why, when Petey relates a newspaper account of the birth of a baby girl, the childless Meg tells him "I'd much rather have a little boy" (I, 11). If the two intruders offer him no better future,

Meg usurps from him the present world outside the 'Panopticon' of her house. To Meg, Stanley's past is dead and she completely denies it when she talks to others about Stanley's social identity in the past. She talks in such a manner as if she is referring to a dead person: "He used to work. He used to be a Pianist. In a concert party on the Pier." (I, 31) Stanley fulfills Meg's desire by playing the role of a sometimes agreeable and sometimes a naughty child. In turn Meg offers him an open and completely uncritical affirmation of his existence. This affirmation is pre-logical and pre-social. The account of Stanley's history as a concert pianist who had a successful concert and then had been locked out of his next is a dim past. We do not know whether it is true or not but one thing, certain about him, is that he feels rejected by the eternal world and so he is afraid of its categories, such as 'successful.' In Meg's dilapidated house, there is no such judgment of the external world. So, a purely subjective, personal affirmation of his identity is given to him by Meg. Steven H. Gale rightly writes, Meg "has no true grasp of the meaning of most words and so, although she talks and listens, she says and hears nothing which bears on life as a meaningful experience" (42). This completely personal assurance of another person ensures Stanley's security. It is suggestive of a child's reaction to the world, implying no firm grip on external reality. We, the common social people, as changing and growing beings relate to the external world in many ways—subjectively and objectively, and in doing so we have to get multiple assurances of our complex identity. To Stanley, they are—personal (Meg), sexual (Lulu) and social (Goldberg and Mccann).

We get the first objective view of Stanley from Lulu's entrance as she urges him to wash himself and to go out from this boarding house to the outer world:

> LULU (offering him the compact). Do you want to have a look at your face? (Stanley withdraws from the table.) You could shave, do you know that? (Stanley sits, right at the table.) Don't you ever go out? (He does not answer.) I mean, what do you do,

just sit around the house like this all day long? (Pause.) Hasn't Mrs. Boles got enough to do without having you under her feet all day long?

STANLEY. I always stand on the table when she sweeps the floor.

LULU. Why don't you have a wash? You look terrible.

STANLEY. A wash wouldn't make any difference.

LULU (rising). Come out and get a bit of air. You depressed me, looking like that. (I, 25-26)

Stanley's attempt to shave later suggests that he himself has a dormant desire to get the touch of the outer world and so shaving is his subconscious recognition of Lulu's demand. But he does not have enough courage to run with the inevitable change of time, hence he denies his birthday. Getting form Meg his birthday gift—a toy drum he suffers from an oscillation between his past and present. The substitution of piano by the toy drum actually substitutes his artistic identity and as an artist one can never admit it. So, he has not played it, rather I should say, he has beat it. That is why, his first drumbeat is regular and then gradually becomes "erratic, uncontrolled" and finally "savage and possessed" (I, 36). This is a symbolic outlet of the stifled forces of the suppressed desire for adult recognition and identity. It is similar to Pinter's own comment in his 'Programme Note for *The Caretaker*': "The more acute the experience the less articulate its expression." (Qtd. Brown 41) This desire for social recognition is first represented obliquely by the anecdote of his concert performance. But by the 'savage,' 'uncontrolled' and 'possessed' pounding of the toy drum it is reduced in scope but magnified in intensity.

Generally, a toy drum is given to the child to help him to derive self-confidence so that in his grown-up age he can master the more complex instrument such as piano. Stanley's confidence was shattered in the past by the social rejection and now Meg has been reinforcing this sense of impotence upon him again and again for over a year. So, it is a tug-of-war between Meg and the intruders and being a rope Stanley is shattered by their hauling up. I cannot completely agree with William Baker and Stephen Tabachnick (though to some extent it is right and suitable for our argument) because of their specific interpretation of the play as a *bar mitzvah.*[3] Here Stanley's ordeal by Goldberg and Mccann before entering into the adult world is compared with the puberty rites almost universally associated with coming to adulthood. Such rites employ a challenge for the boy to overcome before entering into the adult community.

To make Stanley worthy of the adult world Goldberg and Mccann have taken away both the present and the past of Stanley and abandoned him in the midst of 'nowhere.' Now Stanley has no identity and he can only react like an animal with physical action and preliterate sound. This condition fulfills Meg's desire for him as an infant boy and so she passes an ironic comment, "he's my Stanley now. And I think he is a good boy, although sometimes he's bad" (II, 55).

The ending of act I suggests the outlet of forces suppressed by personal identity. Similarly, in the closure of act II, when Stanley has just been deprived of all but the social identity, he attempts desperately to give vent to the other frustrated forces. It is his attempt to undercut the social identity by purely antisocial acts of strangling Meg and raping Lulu. There is a similar parallel between the gifts presented to Stanley by the agents of two identities. Goldberg and Mccann offer Stanley promises of spare tires, club cars, season tickets, crash helmets, yachts and animals. They are the gifts of the adult's world just as the toy drum in the child's world.

From this discussion we get two equally impossible alternatives which never go together. They together can make the self integrated, but separately they can only deny the essential part of one's being. The personal and uncritical assurance of Meg's seaside resort negates Stanley's socio sexual identity and would try to keep him a child forever. On the contrary, the alternative power—of whose agents are the two strangers—spreads its hand to lead one to a new horizon of social identity. But it also allows no personal identity. So, the plight of Stanley is not merely that he is a prey to the frightening figure of Goldberg and Mccann, but his actual predicament is that, between the subjective and social versions of a self, nothing offers the full identity. The play ends by making a complete circle of Stanley's life. Stanley's vague past is just like the dark, inscrutable atmosphere of the womb, his present in the shabby, dilapidated house is nothing but a life of a fallen Adam and his final journey wearing a black suit with two agents has a semblance with the voyage to the Ocean of death. So, it is a circle of life and death, the banal flow of tide and time, where nobody cares who goes and who remains. So, Meg, in the last scene, reduces all that has happened to a purely personal experience:

> MEG. Wasn't it a lovely party last night? . . . It was a lovely party. I haven't laughed so much for years. We had dancing and singing. And games. You should have been there.
> PETEY. It was good, eh?
> Pause.
> MEG. I was the belle of the ball.
> PETEY. Were you?
> MEG. Oh yes. They all said I was.
> PETEY. I bet you were, too.
> MEG. Oh, it's true. I was.
> Pause.
> I know I was. (III, 87).

Psychoanalysis

Now we look at the play from a new point of view which is different from the previous perspective of making identities. It is somehow more deep-rooted and it takes part in making consciousness. It is the plane of psychological archetypes where Meg's motherly affection has been contaminated with her senile eroticism. This type of irregular thinking first pokes our mind when Meg gets delight in Stanley's ascribing the adjective 'succulent' upon Meg's fried bread and, by extension, Meg. Then the sexual tension generated again when we see Meg returning out of breath from Stanley's bed room after waking him. Again, on that time, we find her rearranging hair. There might happen something perverse in the waking scene between the mother and the son. Stanley later reprimands her, saying that she ought not "come into a man's bedroom and—wake him up". (I, 18) Here the hesitation is evocatively present, suggesting that he thinks again about the repeating details of the manner in which Stanley was disturbed.

Stanley is here reluctant to leave the warm, cozy but temporary and seedy shelter built by Meg for him. It may be also taken as the death-drive which draws one toward a lazy, inactive state. Stanley is afraid not only of the outside world in the womb-like sea-side resort of Meg, but also of the fervent attraction of sexuality outside the cozy mother-son relationship. This is suggestive of Stanley's passive sexuality. So, Stanley's effete response to Lulu's vague come-on is in both senses of the phrase: having a girlfriend and going out into the world. We may also view that Stanley's 'washout' offer to take Lulu 'nowhere' clearly conveys the ineffectiveness and sterility of him. From here, we begin to have another cause of his strangling Meg. The cause is that—Meg cannot oppose the destruction of their relationship for her ignorance of the true meaning of the presence of Goldberg and Mccann. In this light, we have to analyze Stanley's attempt to rape Lulu. Goldberg's seductive love play with Lulu is very much provocative for Stanley as it happens in his presence. By it, Stanley has been driven away from his infantile sexuality and he is now under a process of being pushed into the adulterated world. Hence the heinous attempt to rape his own girlfriend/That's why, he has attempted to rape.

The whole situation may also be viewed as Stanley's severing the ties of maternity and gentle sexuality. Taking it into consideration, we may see Meg's birthday gift of a boy's drum as a visual umbilical cord between Meg and Stanley. It also associates

Stanley to womanhood in general, beyond Meg, as it is Lulu who brings the gift for Stanley. So, when he puts his foot through the drum skin, we apprehend this is nothing but a hymen-breaking action which cuts the maternal bond between Stanley and Meg as well as Stanley and his motherly feelings.

Sigmund Freud in his 1914 essay 'On Narcissism: an introduction' (*Penguin Freud Library*, vol. XI) found the two levels of libido—ego-libido and object-libido. An infant of the age of six months remains completely entangled in its world of hunger, thirst, sleep. So, it is fully disorganized due to its necessity and helplessness. Freud calls it ego-libido but as he grows up, he gradually learns to connect his libido with certain things or any person of the outside world. It actually drives the child towards another person or another thing to fill up the void or the lack within it. So, it is a process of making the self. This libido is object-libido. And this mechanism of transformation from ego-libido to object-libido is called Cathexis. Freud calls this stage of ego-libido of the infant—Primary Narcissism.

Stanley in *The Birthday Party* is the incarnation of the Primary Narcissism. This whole process of Cathexis is completely and very evidently seen in his character. His infantile existence under the shade of the motherly affection of Meg is clearly reflective of his ego-libido. For this reason, he takes Lulu 'nowhere.' The crisis period of his life is its first step towards object-libido. Lulu is his first object. But due to his Primary Narcissism, he cannot accomplish his Cathexis accurately. So, he needs the two intruders. In this stage of Primary Narcissism, the consciousness or the self has no centre. Freud, in his *Metapsychology*, says, "I may point out that we are bound to suppose that a unity comparable to ego cannot exist in the individual from the start; the ego has to be developed" (69). Goldberg and Mccann help him to develop his ego. In this respect Martin Esslin is very apt to say: "Seen from this angle, Stanley's removal in the garb of the respectable hardworking suburban breadwinner would be an image of the adult's nostalgic leave-taking from the cozy, comfortable, warm, cared-for world of his childhood, his view of the adult world as one of Adam driven out from Paradise to earn his daily dread by the sweat of his brow." (*Pinter The Playwright* 75).

The play may also be taken as a paragon of oedipal syndrome. Meg is here depicted as a mother figure with her subconscious incestuous yearning to his child-like Stanley who also has a Suppressed desire of making sex with her. Thus, Stanley has an oedipal wish and he gets indulgence from Meg. So here Stanley's fear of the avenging angels emitted from 'the organization' may be symbolic of his guilt feelings for his illicit incestuous impulses. It implies Stanley's frightened situation due to his dread of punishment of the father figure. This father is not only the supreme power of the patriarchal society. Rather, "It is in the *name of the father* that we must recognize the basis of the symbolic function which, since the dawn of historical time, has identified his person with the figure of the law" (Lacan, *Ecrits* 231). Here the father figure has been drawn in the character of Goldberg with his one-man army, Mccann. Goldberg, with his exaggerated Jewish family feelings, has a father like appearance. So, he has come to take his revenge upon Stanley. In this context, we comprehend the symbol of Mccann's habit of tearing strips out of newspapers. It is now clearly the projection of castration fear. Thus, the persecution allotted to Stanley is originally the punishment attributed to the perverted wishers. Stanley probably anticipates it, so he suffers from the persecution mania of a neurotic refugee throughout the whole play. So, the escorting of Stanley to Monty is nothing but sending him to an asylum to make him a 'mensch' and maybe its description we can get from his next drama *The Hothouse*. Hence, we can conclude from this discussion that this play does not any psychoanalysis of its characters, rather the play is psychoanalysis per se.

Conclusion

In the previous five consecutive sub-chapters, we have different meanings and analyses of the play. But they are not the all. There are a number of explanations and meanings in it. I have given only those which I can think of. For example, to make a 'mensch' out of Stanley may also be seen as a theme of birth or rebirth regarding Stanley. It will not be a hyperbole if I call it a postmodern sub-version of the reconciliation motif of birth and regeneration that usually served as a closure in Shakespearean tragicomedy. In Shakespeare's *The Tempest* Ferdinand's symbolic demise, trial and induction into higher mysteries guide to a rebirth with the promises of reconciliation, wedding and new empire. Such an ending of the Elizabethan drama was an aberration that created a contradiction. In the modern and also to some extent in the postmodern arena, the existential dramas had done away with such garbs and here the closure of the drama openly faces the crisis. Hence the protagonist, here, is promised a rebirth as a 'new man' fit for the society by the emissaries of the civilized, adulterated world, not by Providence.

The style of the play is also like a mystery-thriller or a detective fiction. But finally, it does not adhere long to the generic relation of a mystery-thriller. In a mystery-thriller, many explanations of events may for a time being, seem equally feasible. But after a certain time, all false possibilities gradually begin to shade from our mind and once single, resolute meaning begins to prevail. But in *The Birthday Party*, we never come to know the true reason for the fear; instead, we have been left amidst the make-believe possibilities. So, whereas the detective fiction or the mystery-thriller emphasizes upon the enlightenment focus of the triumph of reason over chaos, in this play the interrogation of Stanley underscores the evasion of reason rather than its assertion. So, though here we have the glimpses of a mystery-thriller in the beginning and the middle of the play, yet actually Pinter wants to make a parody of its effect at the end. Ultimately the playwright subsumes it to the 'mixed mood' of a pastiche.

Thus, *The Birthday Party* of Harold Pinter is a play where the enigma of meanings leads the audience to a problematic situation. But the main problem of Stanley in the play is his lack of communication. Had he expressed properly what he actually was and was not—then he would not have faced the two tormentors. Then the play would have been another play with a 'sensitive intellectual' articulate hero. So, our search for meaning here is futile. The letter of the playwright himself to Peter Wood very clearly justifies it:

Meaning begins in the words, in action, continues in your head and ends nowhere. There is no end to meaning. Meaning which is resolved, parceled, labeled and ready for export is dead, impertinent—and meaningless. I examine my own play and ask, what's going on here? I note—this seems to lead from that, I would conclude this, but the characters themselves do nothing but move through an occurrence, a morning, a night, a morning. This occurrence has, admittedly, any number of implications. Anyone is entitled to see the show. The dramatic progression and the implications implicit in it will either find a home in some part of their nut or not. (Casebook 80).

NOTES

1. It is a term popularized by poet and critic T.S. Eliot in his famous essay "Hamlet and His Problems" refers to actions, objects or situations that correspond with and thus implicitly evoke a particular emotion from the audience or reader.
2. As a literary term, it is associated with Soviet critic Mikhail Bakhtin and with dialogic criticism, a method of literary criticism based on Bakhtin's theories.
3. In the Jewish religion, a boy attains the age (usually 13 years) of religious responsibility; the festivities held in recognition of this event are called *bar mitzvah.*

The Enigmatic Identities of the Characters in *The Room*

In the plays of Pinter's first phase, a striking language of violence and menace prevails. In the first phase, the context is also the human relationship among the assailants and the victims. The unknown agents of this violence are of unverifiable origin. They are the elemental signs of menace. It confuses the identity of the characters. The human forms which are used to dramatize the menace are not ready with logic of motivation. In a drama, plot, action and dialogue are being moved by a centripetal force related to the character. Character is an abstraction felt from the pattern of this relatedness. This abstraction is made concrete on the stage by the living actor. The drama may be very much symbolic or allegorical, but the dramatic character always turns up as a distinctive human being. In Pinter's dramas of the fifties, to create an ambiance of fear and incertitude, the characters are very simply manipulated. It leads to the existential fear of selfhood slipping away from one's grip. In contemporary times, there is an extensive treatment of this theme.

In the present chapter, I want to illuminate a different aspect of the politics involved by Pinter's characters. Here I take the short one-act play *The Room* to show how the different identities of the individual characters subvert the meaning of the whole play as well as the predominant discourse of the play. It reflects that truth becomes a matter of personal perception, that truth becomes relative and so is the identity.

> ROSE: What's it like out?
> MRS SANDS: It's very dark out.
> MR SANDS: No darker than in. (97)

Naturalism in drama has demystified reality. In plays like *The Room*, instead of pride and jealousy, fear is the prime 'flaw,' imparting to the play a psychological orientation. The characters here suffer from the horror and skepticism every moment of his existence, but in the plays, there is no indication of the evasion of it. The characters in the play are seen in a familiar situation, but they seem unpredictable and idiosyncratic in their reactions. Their fear and doubt sometimes do not facilitate logical, normal responses. This type of play, therefore, seems inconsequential. In this way, the characters in *The Room* can be conveyed through long stretches of confusion and violence leading nowhere in particular.

Generally, death is accepted by a common man as a crucial moment of transition, as a junction between time and eternity. But to the postmodern writers the journey of the soul, as well as the self, begins and ends in this temporal world. Here is no illusion of the after-life existence and so naturally no prospect of serving a God. In the absence of such faith, here the individual tries his best 'to drink the life to the lees' and in doing so the 'little man' struggles to transcend his 'trivial,' short life in his consciousness. He attempts to make 'his little room everywhere,' to make his home the heaven. But when this great attempt of the trivial man fails, the self ceases to exist. Actually, the self-negating force is the agent of violence; it is an embodiment of nothingness. The individual is frightened of this nothingness. It is actually the projection of the fear of losing everything—the relationship, the abode. Likewise, in *The Room*, the assailants may be nothing but simply the externalization of the psychological menace of the victim.

To analyze the different levels of identity of the characters of *The Room*, we first take in consideration the character of the victim or the female protagonist Rose. Rose has a dual self. Her speech in the play informs us that she is the wife of Mr. Bert Hudd. "My husband's in his van. He doesn't drive slow either." (98) The second sentence of the quotation has not any direct relation with the first; rather it implies a psycho-sexuality. Ten years Bert

Hudd's senior, Rose is not the mother of Bert, but she is his wife. But her action and affection towards her husband confounded us whether she is Bert's wife or mother. The way she tries to satisfy him reminds us of a mother coaxing her child: "Rose isn't a mother, but she's the prototype of all Pinter's chattering, fussing, nagging mother-figures, the women who never stop to listen but never stop asking implicitly for the good-will of the husband or son or nephew or lodger." (Hayman 1970: 11)

On the other hand, in the opening scene, we find Rose continuing to prattle on about the food, the dress, the room, about this and that. Bert makes no reply. Here the audience is prepared to get the notion that what this vocalization of Rose and the taciturnity of Bert imply is that Rose is being refused by her husband to be given any reassurance or dominance. When Rose asks a question to Bert, she either replies it herself or simply bypasses it to get at any other issue. It is clearly indicative of an undercurrent of tension in the relationship of this wife with his rude husband. This incident we can interpret in two ways. First, here the words are delivered in such a way that we can say that Rose, nevertheless, knows that Bert is neglecting her. But as Rose hardly gives Bert any time to answer, it can be said that the wife also wants to belittle her spouse equally.

Rose praises her room as a warm and secure place, and looks down upon the outside world as dark, cold and hostile. To her the room provides safety from the inimical outer world. But the room cannot be called completely secure. Bernard F. Dukore gives a wonderful metaphor in this regard: "Despite its resemblance to rhyming alternatives, *The Room* differs from The Tomb which permits no exit, and *The Womb* which permitting no entry, is entirely secure. Nor is *The Room* the same as *The Home*, which might suggest ownership or belonging." (28)

However, Rose never leaves the room and not only that, she becomes very anxious whenever Bert goes out of the room. Again, contrary to what Dukore says, the room is like a womb that ensures care and protection for its inhabitants and here Rose wants to function as a womb for Bert. Her maternal instinct is evidently identified with her love for the room: "This is a good room. You've got a chance in a place like this. I look after you, don't I, Bert? Like when they offered us the basement here I said no straight off. I knew that'd be no good. The ceiling right on top of you. No, you've got a window here, you can move yourself." (89)

Eugene Ionesco's famous play *The Chairs* has an Old Man and an Old Woman who have spent their 'seventy-five years of married life.' The Old Woman has the same dual identity, as she is characterized as a wife/mother archetype like Rose. She is more like an old mother than a spouse to her husband. When the Old Man is in tension, the Old Woman provides him courage. "Mummy's with you, what are you afraid of?" (Ionesco 132). The Old Man can recognize the basis of this fundamental relationship and hence he is reciprocal unlike Bert Hudd. "My worthy spouse, semiramis has taken the place of my mother" (Ionesco 148).

But in this play, the affectionate wife Rose never gets such acknowledgement from her husband. Bert here remains taciturn and sullen. He hides himself behind the magazine. Rose does not stop talking as she doesn't mind the insulting slighting of Bert like a loving mother who does not pay attention to her petulant child.

Now I want to illumine the various traits of another central character of the play, that is, the blind Negro Riley. He is the most interesting character in the play. His character may be viewed from four perspectives. He may be the on-stage projection of Rose's fear, may be the ghost figure, may be the victim of racial segregation and finally he may also be the redemptive figure. As the play is open-ended, the playwright leaves the onus of identifying him to the audience. This dark blind man appears towards the end of the play, and from that moment the play takes a 179-degree turn from this mundane, real human world and conjures the surreal, mysterious world. Before his entrance the couple leads their conjugal life peacefully. But their sense of safety and peacefulness is so fragile and ephemeral that even a single knock on the door can collapse their feeling of integration, and they are engulfed by a nameless menace and foreboding. They have not any acquaintance with the other tenants in the other floors of the building and even they do not know whether there is any other tenant or not. They do not have the accurate knowledge of the landlord also. They live a completely isolated life of their own and want to carry it on.

> MR. SANDS. Yes, I know it is. But Mrs. Hudd seems to know Mr. Kidd very well.
> ROSE. No, I wouldn't say that. As a matter of fact, I don't know him at all. We're very quiet. We keep ourselves to ourselves. I never interfere. I mean, why should I? We've got our room. We don't bother anyone else. That's the way it should be. (99)

Rose is frightened of the dark and wet basement and also of the thinking of the cold, hostile outside. Actually, her intense fear takes the shape of a black human-being who, she suspects, has come to evict her from her haven. So Riley is none but an incarnation of her own fear coming from her subconscious. Thus, Riley may be called an embodiment of certain sinister surreal or non-human forces. Therefore, he cannot fulfill the conventional expectations about a character.

The second identity of Riley as the ghost figure is basically given by Martin Esslin. To Esslin, Riley is not only a messenger from Rose's father, but he himself is Sal's father.

> RILEY. Your father wants you to come home.
> *Pause.*
> ROSE. Home?
> RILEY. Yes.
> ROSE. Home? Go now. Come on. It's late. It's late.
> RILEY. To come home.
> ROSE. Stop it. I can't take it. What do you want? What do you want?
> RILEY. Come home, Sal. (108)

Riley's comment "your father wants you to come home" transforms after a few moments into "I want you to come home" (108). It clearly creates a surreal atmosphere. The light of the room, the darkness of the basement and the outside together create, in this atmosphere, a chiaroscuro effect of Rembrandt Van Rijn. In this situation, it is natural for a spectator to think Riley as the spirit of a dead man—the spirit of Rose's dead father. Martin Esslin, in this context, aptly comments: "The blind Negro, on the other hand, who has been lying in the basement for days and who appears to bring Rose a message from her past, is all too manifestly a symbol, an allegory. He has been lying down below and had foreknowledge of the future—that room number seven would soon be vacant—he must therefore be a being from beyond the confines of this world: a dead man or a messenger of death, perhaps Rose's own dead father. His blackness and his blindness reinforce these allegorical implications. The blindness which strikes Rose at the end belongs to the same category of symbolism—it must mean the end of her relationship with Bert, but probably more than that: her own death." (57)

Another important side of Riley's identity is his ethnic or racial origin. Riley in his appearance and name represents the two ethnic identities—Black and Irish. They both suffer from racial oppression by the Whites. In post-war Britain, they are commonly excluded from tenancy rights. Hence to beat such a racially marginalized man brutally by a British in his own country is not a very unnatural incident in the xenophobic England of 1950s. In 1957, racism, fascism emerged in England through the party of Enoch Powell set in opposition against the immigration population and the open immigration policy of Britain. So, the final scene of killing or injuring the Negro can never be devoid of political resonance at a time of great social unease over issues of race and immigration.

But this final situation can be narrated from another standpoint. Rose does not want to reveal her identity; she wants to obliterate her past. Probably she had done something wrong and she earnestly wants to conceal it. Pinter shows in this play how a modern man is afraid of allowing others to peep into his deeply buried self. So, we can also say that Bert attacks the Negro not out of racial hatred but because Bert suspects that Riley has known some confidential information relating to the past life of his wife and this information gives the Negro a peculiar power over Rose. Here Bert is not seen as a criminal, but as a protector returned to safeguard their hearth and home.

All the above interpretations locate Riley as a harbinger of evil forces. But all these readings are refuted by Pinter himself in one of his rare discussions. If we look at Pinter's own life, we will see that Pinter wrote *The Room* only six weeks after his marriage. Pinter loved his parents and was loved by his parents very much. Going outside the Jewish faith of his family, he married Vivian Merchant (to whom the published text was dedicated) upon his parents. It resulted in an immediate break with the Thistlewaite Road of his upbringing where he largely spent his first twenty-five years. I do not agree with Michael Billington who is not ready to accept that *The Room* is "a projection of his own guilt about the emotional dislocation caused by his marriage and his fear that the insistent claims of the family, of tradition and the past are never that easily put aside—a theme to which he constantly returns." (69) I think Rose's character is the shadow of Pinter himself and Riley is therefore nobody but projection of Pinter's own dead father, his lost paternal love. This reading is justified by Pinter's own comment as he has seen Riley "as a messenger, a potential savior who is trying to release Rose from the imprisonment of the room and the restrictions of her life with Bert. He's inviting her to come back to her spiritual home; which is why he gets beaten up when Bert returns. But, to me, Riley has always been a redemptive figure and that was how I staged it when I later came to direct it with Vivien and a fine black actor called Thomas Baptiste." (qtd. Billington 69)

In this chapter we should not avoid the discussion about the minor character Mr. Kidd who can play well with his identity. He is the possible landlord of the room. He is neither a kid nor an old man in his intelligence. Rather he is a very clever person. His conversation with Rose has a very subtle politics. Here the language of communication is not present. One cannot apply the appropriate speeches to the appropriate identities. We have to gather meaning from the linguistic gaps.

> ROSE. What about your sister, Mr. Kidd?
> MR. KIDD. What about her?
> ROSE. Did she have any babies?
> MR. KIDD. Yes, she had a resemblance to my old mum, I think. Taller, of course.
> ROSE. When did she kill your sister?
> MR. KIDD. Yes, that's right, it was after she died that I must have stopped counting. . . .
> ROSE. What did she die of?
> MR. KIDD. Who?
> ROSE. Your sister.
> Pause.
> MR. KIDD. I've made ends meet. (93)

Here the questions do not have the direct answers. But what we get from this conversation is the constant evasion of points. Here linguistic non communication can be used as a fence or a smokescreen behind the cover of which Kidd wants to conceal his identity. Kidd does not want to expose himself as a Jew in the world of Auschwitz. So, he willingly invests an uncertainty into his identity. "I think my mum was a Jewess. Yes, I wouldn't be surprised to learn that she was a Jewess." (93) Underneath this incertitude he wants to conceal what his Jewish name exposes—his Jewish blood.

From the above discussions in this chapter, we perceive that Pinter's characters represent man's fear, his inadequacies, his longings and motivations—both known and unknown. Pinter surprisingly uses here the unverifiability of the characters as a component of realism to obfuscate the audience. His enigmatic and unpredictable characters in this play remain always elusive. They are just like the strangers we suddenly come across in a train or in a shop. We can never completely understand their motives. To create a certain poignant seriousness, the characters bring together the non-rational and natural behavior in a familiar situation and in this way *coup de theatre*[2] of great impact has been produced. The politics of identity in Pinter's characters suggests that the apparently knowable is always remote and strange in essentials. So, one can never relate Pinter's characters to an off-stage reality because the reason for the odd behavior of his character (for example, Bert's attacking Riley) is buried in a dim past that does not exist outside the text and their psychology. Ronald Hayman very precisely exposes the subtle qualitative differences between the vagueness of the characters of Pinter and that of Samuel Beckett: "Beckett's characters are vague above time and place, but the vagueness is apparently involuntary. They seem genuinely unable to provide each other with information about their present situation or about recent events in their experience or current event in the world outside. Pinter's characters are equally vague and uncommunicative, but it does not always seem that ignorance is their reason for withholding information. They tend to be less benevolent, more competitive, aggressive, perverse. They are liable to provide misleading information for the sake of causing confusion and anxiety, disturbing the audience at the same time as they disturb each other. Pinter constantly violates the theatrical convention by which audiences can assume that characters are truthful unless clear indications are given to it." (126)

NOTE

1. It is a sudden and sensational turn in a play to arouse a theatrical effect.

Conclusion

Harold Pinter has created an integrated pattern of words and gesture, of the realistic and the symbolic to suggest the inexpressible stasis of human condition. Pinter employs more words and more movements than Beckett. Pinter's plays, from *The Room* to *The Homecoming,* are not plot-centric, rather they are event centered and the events are ordered haphazardly as in real life, not according to any causal plan. In Pinter's plays the thematic development is not so important; as politics is involved in each conversation and situation, there is always the plotting of psychological compulsions. To explore the politics of the situation and the identity of the individual, Pinter projects the complex psychological states of modern life by using low-life idiom and conversational speech. The duration of his play is so small and the description of the past happening is so little that one can never accurately analyze the present action. One can only realize the politics involved in the situation. Pinter selects events and characters not from history and mythology because history and mythology always represent the politics of a totalitarian society, not of the individuals. To locate the identity of the individual and the politics of the interpersonal relationship Pinter exploits the banality of human existence.

The audience cannot fully understand the condition in which Pinter's character has been trapped; probably the characters themselves do not fully understand it. The politics of the situation actually bewilders the characters as well as the audience and it also creates the enigma of identity of the characters for the audience. Joseph Melancon's remark is relevant in this regard: "Keeping the character in the dark about former events already known by the audience is the source of the blunders and mistaken identities which have been put to good use by the theatre of the past have been reversed. Now the audience is kept in the dark about the former events either already known by the character or not known to him at all." (22)

Here the audience has a little information of the character's past. So according to their own personal apprehension which, they themselves know, perhaps is not reliable, the audience creates the identities of the characters in their mind. No single perspective is thus sufficient to properly appreciate the identities of Pinter's characters. The present work has shown in the previous chapters how Pinter's characters try to hide their identity and cast illusory images of themselves. Sometimes they consciously avoid and sometimes they are mentally unable to come to grip with one's own identity. That is why the characters play the language game of pretence to create an illusory identity and in this way, they desperately try to escape from the barbarity and isolation of their own lives. So, to realize the politics entangled in these 'history-less' character's identity a multi-perspectival approach is essential.

This multi-perspectival approach leads the audience to the enigma of the plurality of meanings. All this boils down to the conclusion that univocality and uniformity of a text is an illusion. Cartesian myth of a stable self or a fixed identity, in this personal yet political world, has no empirical foundation. The playwright just like any other human being, is a jumble of confused and contradictory emotions and a text being polysemantic, its space is always inhabited by a multiplicity of meanings.

Bibliography

Almansi, Guido and Simon Henderson. *Harold Pinter.* Ed. Malcolm Bradbury and Christopher Bigsby. London: Methuen, 1983.

Baker, William. *Harold Pinter.* London: Continuum, 2008.

Batty, Mark. *Harold Pinter*. New Delhi: Atlantic, 2010.

Beckett, Samuel. *Waiting for Godot*. London: Faber, 1968.

Berne, Eric. *Games People Play*. Harmondsworth: Penguin, 1968.

Billington, Michael. *The Life and Work of Harold Pinter.* London: Faber, 1997.

Bloom, Harold. *Harold Pinter: Modern Critical Views.* New York: Chelsea House,1987.

Brooke, Nicholas. *Horrid Laughter in Jacobean Tragedy*. London: Open Books, 1979.

Brown, John R. *Theatre Language: A Study of Arden, Osborne, Pinter and Wesker*. New York: Taplinger, 1972.

Cahn, Victor. Gender and Power in the Plays of Harold Pinter, New York: St. Martin's Press, 1993.

Camus, Albert. *The Myth of Sisyphus,* trans. M. Edward. London: Penguin, 1973.

Chaudhury, Sukanta, ed. *A Certain Sense: Poems by Jibananda Das*, trans. Chaudhury et al. New Delhi: Sahitya Akademi, 2002.

Dukore, Bernard F. *Harold Pinter.* London: Macmillan, 1988.

_____. *Where Laughter Stops: Pinter's Tragicomedy.* Columbia and London: University of Missouri Press, 1976.

Dutton, Richard. *Modern tragicomedy and the British Tradition: Beckett, Pinter, Stoppard, Albee and Storey.* Sussex: Harvester Press, 1986.

Eliot, T.S. "Ulysses, Order and Myth". *Selected Prose of T.S. Eliot*, ed. Frank Kermode. London: Faber, 1975.

Esslin, Martin. *Pinter The Playwright.* 5th ed; London: Methuen, 1992.

_____. *The Theatre of the Absurd*. 3rd ed. London: Methuen, 2001.

Foucault, Michel. *Power/ Knowledge: Selected Interviews and Other Writings, 1972-1977*, ed. Colin Gordon. Trans. Colin Gordon, Leo Marshall, John Mepham, Kate Soper. Sussex: Harvester Press, 1980.

Freud, Sigmund. "On Metapsychology". *Penguin Freud Library*, ed. Angela Richards. Vol.11. London: Penguin, 1984.

Gabbard, Lucina Paquet. *The Dream Structure of Pinter's Plays: A Psychoanalytic Approach.* Cranbury: Associated University Press, 1976.

Gale, Steven H. *Butter's Going up: A Critical Analysis of Harold Pinter's Work.* Durham, N. C.: Duke University Press, 1977.

Ganz, Arthur. *Realms of the Self: Variations on a Theme in Modern Drama.* New York and London: New York University Press, 1980.

Gelb, Arthur and Barbara Eds. *O' Neill*. New York: Dell, 1965.

Hall, Peter. "A Director's Approach". *A Casebook on Harold Pinter's The Homecoming*, ed. John and Antha Lahr. New York: Grove Press, 1971.

Hayman, Ronald. *Harold Pinter*. London: Heinemann, 1970.

_____. "Pinter and Stoppard". *Theatre and Anti-Theatre: New Movements Since Beckett.* New York: Oxford Univ. Press, 1979.

Hinchcliffe, Arnold P. *British Theatre, 1950-1970.* Oxford: Basil Blackwell, 1974.

_____. *Harold Pinter*. New York: Twayne, 1967.

Hutchinson, Peter. "Games with The Readers", *Games Authors Play*. London: Methuen, 1983.

Ionesco, Eugene. "The Chairs". *Penguin Plays*. Trans. Donald Watson. England: Penguin, 1973.

Jenkins, John. Brodie's Notes on Harold Pinter's *The Birthday Party*, *The Caretaker* and *The Homecoming*, ed. Graham Handley. London: Macmillan, 1998.

Kafka, Franz. *The Trial.* Delhi: Surjeet, 2006.

Lacan, Jacques. "The Subversion of the Subject and the Dialectic of Desire in the Freudian Unconscious". *Ecrits*, trans. Bruce Fink, Heloise Fink and Russel Grigg. New York: Norton, 2006.

_____. "The Function and Field of Speech and Language in Psychoanalysis". *Ecrits*, trans. Bruce Fink, Heloise Fink and Russel Grigg.

Lahiri, Pradip. *Harold Pinter: A Study in Dialogic Art*. New Delhi: Prestige, 1996.

Lahr, John and Antha, ed. *A Casebook on Harold Pinter's The Homecoming.* New York: Grove Press, 1971.

Lloyd Evans, Gareth and Barbara Eds. *Plays in Review, 1956-1980.* London: Batsford Academic and Educational, 1985.

Melancon, Joseph. "Theatre as Semiotic Practice", trans. Paul Perron, *Modern Drama*. Vol. 25, No. 1, March, 1982.

Naismith, Bill. *A Faber Critical Guide: Harold Pinter*. London: Faber, 2000.

Pinter, Harrold. *Plays: One.* London: Faber, 1976.

_____. *Plays: Three.* London: Faber, 1978.

_____. *The Birthday Party.* London: Faber, 1991.

_____. "A Letter to Peter Wood". *Harold Pinter: A Casebook.* Ed. Michael Scott. Houndmills: Macmillan, 1986.

_____. "A View of the Party". *Harold Pinter: A Casebook.* Ed. Michael Scott. Houndmills: Macmillan, 1986.

_____. "Harold Pinter: Nobel Lecture: Art, Truth & Politics." www.nobelprize.org/nobel_prizes/literature/laureates/2005/pinter-lecture-e.html

Rogers, Paul. "An Actor's Approach". *A Casebook on Harold Pinter's The Homecoming*, ed. John and Antha Lahr. New York: Grove Press, 1971.

Scott, Michael, ed. *Harold Pinter: A Casebook.* Houndmills: Macmillan, 1986.

Silverstein, Marc. *Harold Pinter and the Language of Cultural Power*. London: Associated University Press, 1993.

Supple, Barry. 'Pinter's Homecoming,' *Jewish Chronicle* (25 June 1965): 7, 31.

Trussler, Simon. *The Plays of Harold Pinter: An Assessment*. London: Victor Gollancz, 1973.

Wardle, Irving. "The Territorial Struggle". *A Casebook on Harold Pinter's The Homecoming.* Eds. John and Antha Lahr. 40-44.

Wilson, Edwin. *The Theatre Experience.* 5th ed. Toronto: McGraw Hill, 1991.

Worth, Katherine J. "Pinter and the Realist Tradition". *Harold Pinter: A Casebook.* Ed. Michael Scott. Houndmills: Macmillan, 1986.